D0765432

Praise for *Hound Dog*

"One of the greatest songwriting teams in pop history . . . finally tells its story. . . . Together they come up with one of the more breezily entertaining music books in years."

—R. J. Smith, *Los Angeles Times*

"Their remarkable story is long overdue."

—Andy Greene, *Rolling Stone*

"Leiber and Stoller were among the pioneers who helped bring black and white musical forms together. It has been a historically fraught process, but the collision of cultures is probably what has given such energy and tension to American music. *Hound Dog* is an important part of that story."

—Jim Windolf, *The New York Times Book Review*

"Leiber and Stoller helped spearhead the transition from R&B to rock in the '50s, going on to compose more hits than any duo not named Lennon and McCartney. . . . The highs and lows of that seminal, soon-to-be-big-business era are catalogued in flamboyant detail in this new, page-turning autobiography. . . . Great insider memories."

—Steve Morse, *The Boston Globe*

"Two big-city boys set out to write the blues. . . . And somehow, they ended up as founding fathers of a new music called rock 'n' roll. . . . *Hound Dog* stands as a compelling piece of oral history."

—Michael E. Young, *The Dallas Morning News*

"Like their best songs, *Hound Dog* is short, snappy, colorful, funny, a little rude . . . and you might even be able to dance to it."

—Steven Gaydos, *Variety*

"Sharp and funny."

—Allen Pierleoni, *The Sacramento Bee*

"A vividly colorful portrait of two wild and cool cats whose dreams could not possibly have been as big as their lives and legacy turned out to be."

—John Kehe, *The Christian Science Monitor*

"Here is a book the world has needed for many decades—Jerry Leiber and Mike Stoller's own story in well-arranged, wildly readable words. Short, punchy, as irresistible as a Leiber/Stoller song. . . . One of the indispensable books of 2009 as well as one of the most rollickingly pleasurable."

—Jeff Simon, *The Buffalo News*

Simon & Schuster Paperbacks
A Division of Simon & Schuster, Inc.
1230 Avenue of the Americas
New York, NY 10020

First Simon & Schuster trade paperback edition June 2010

SIMON & SCHUSTER PAPERBACKS and colophon are registered trademarks
of Simon & Schuster, Inc.

For information about special discounts for bulk purchases,
please contact Simon & Schuster Special Sales at
1-866-506-1949 or business@simonandschuster.com.

The Simon & Schuster Speakers Bureau can bring authors
to your live event. For more information or to book an event,
contact the Simon & Schuster Speakers Bureau
at 1-866-248-3049 or visit our website at www.simonspeakers.com.

Designed by Paul Dippolito

Manufactured in the United States of America

10   9   8   7   6   5   4   3   2   1

The Library of Congress has cataloged the hardcover edition as follows:

Leiber, Jerry.
    Hound dog: the Leiber & Stoller autobiography / Jerry Leiber and
    Mike Stoller with David Ritz.
        p.   cm.
    Includes bibliographical references and index.
    1. Leiber, Jerry. 2. Stoller, Mike. 3. Lyricists—United States—Biography.
4. Composers—United States—Biography. 5. Rock music—United States—
History and criticism. I. Stoller, Mike. II. Ritz, David. III. Title.
ML385.L396 2009
782.42166092'2—dc22
[B]   2008047821
ISBN 978-1-4165-5938-2
ISBN 978-1-4165-5939-9 (pbk)
ISBN 978-1-4165-6680-9 (ebook)

Pages 305–308 constitute an extension of the copyright page.

Hound Dog

The Leiber and Stoller Autobiography

Jerry Leiber

and

Mike Stoller

with David Ritz

Simon & Schuster Paperbacks

NEW YORK   LONDON   TORONTO   SYDNEY

For Corky,
Amy,
Peter & Tricia,
Adam & Sharon
　　—Mike

For Jed,
Oliver, &
Jake
　　—Jerry

In memory of Joel Dorn
　　—David

*Standing (left to right): Lester Sill, Jerry Wexler, The Coasters
(Carl Gardner, Will "Dub" Jones, Billy Guy, Cornell Gunter),
Ahmet Ertegun. Seated: Jerry Leiber, Mike Stoller.*

Contents

You know, gentlemen, no matter how many beautiful songs you write or how many other major achievements you may realize in your lifetimes, you'll always be remembered as the guys who wrote "Hound Dog."

—Nesuhi Ertegun

Hound Dog

East Coast Roots

Leiber   "Hey, man, how 'bout a poke?" I asked.

"Here you go, bruz. Just keep it dry. Know what I mean?"

"Yeah, I know what you mean—dry."

We slapped each other five and laughed. Dunbar was my asshole buddy in life, a black dude who taught me how to fight the Polacks down the street.

Stoller   I slipped in the back door of the barn. I slipped in quietly because I didn't want to be noticed. And I didn't want to disturb the man playing the piano. I was eight years old, at a sleepaway camp in New Jersey, and hearing boogie-woogie for the first time.

The piano player was a black teenager. He seemed to rock with the rhythm as he played a beat-up upright piano. He was playing for himself—playing his heart out. Boogie-woogie was a new and magical world for me. I was instantly in love with it. I wanted to be able to play it and be part of it.

I stood in a dark corner of the barn, hidden from the pianist. I thought if he saw me, he'd stop playing, and I didn't want him ever to stop. I stayed for his entire solo session. Time flew. The flying notes made me dizzy. So much was happening at once.

I can't explain why, but the music was changing me. If sounds could be this exciting, I had to be part of the excitement. Camp was exciting because of the ethnic mix. In 1941, only a strong, politically left-leaning kids' camp would implement the integration of black and white children. Only a strong left-leaning kids' camp would invite Paul Robeson to sing Negro spirituals and Hebrew folk songs. And only a strong left hand could play this boogie-woogie that was changing my life.

Leiber
One afternoon I went to the home of Uncle Dave, who had a large gray stone house in the Druid Hills section of Baltimore. Uncle Dave had always looked down on my dad, a door-to-door milkman who died penniless. He looked down on my mom, and he also looked down on me. Still, Uncle Dave gave students room and board in exchange for small chores, such as giving piano lessons. And I wanted to learn piano.

It was springtime. I ran up the four flights of stairs that led to the attic where he stored an old Bösendorfer upright. Through the panes of the octagonal window, I could see the spreading branches of the great oak tree, alive with green buds. I was alive with green buds, too. I was taken with my teacher, Yetta Schlossberg. She was seriously ugly, but she had the most beautiful gams in Christendom. Her knees were peeping out from the piano. When she crossed them, the sound of nylon rubbing against nylon excited me, even if I was too young to understand why.

"Before we start," said Yetta, sensing my excitement at the sight of her legs, "let me hear a little bit of that boogie-woogie you've been playing."

I tried my best to play boogie-woogie, but I couldn't.

"Try again," said Yetta, "only this time, slow down the tempo a bit. Your left hand is playing faster than your right. It's racing."

I tried again as best I could. A couple of minutes into it, though, the door burst open and there stood my uncle, his eyes popping out of his head and neck veins bulging. Without warning, he violently slammed down the wooden keyboard cover. I almost didn't get my hands away in time. If I hadn't, he would have crippled me.

"Out of my house!" he roared loudly enough for half of Baltimore to hear. "I want you out of here this minute. I give this woman room and board to teach you how to play the piano like a *mensch*, and you reward me with this garbage? These lessons are over. Take this music back to the gutter where you found it!"

Stoller In my home, music symbolized the stratification between my father's and mother's families.

Mom was born in Pittsburgh. Shortly after her mother died, a suicide, my grandfather took his five children off to Vienna, his native city, where he hired a governess and promptly abandoned his family. The governess raised them. Mom's older sister, my aunt Ray, was a musical prodigy who graduated from the Vienna Conservatory at age twelve. She played harpsichord, organ, and piano. When World War I broke out, Travelers Aid sent the children back to Pittsburgh and located my grandfather. A few years later, the five kids wound up living on their own on Riverside Drive in New York City.

My aunt became a concert pianist, and also a recluse. My mother, Adelyn Endore, was quite beautiful, and dated her neighbor George Gershwin. Mom became a model and actress and appeared in the chorus of *Funny Face* on Broadway. In Vienna, she had been fluent in German and French. Except for a smattering of French, those languages were lost to her in America. Later in life, she painted landscapes imbued with haunting loneliness. When scrutinized carefully, those paintings could point to the great crucible of her life: a debilitating depression that was undoubtedly rooted in her trying childhood.

My mother married my father, Abe Stoller, during the Great Depression. My sister, Joanne, was born in 1929; I was born in Belle Harbor, Queens, in 1933, a few weeks before Jerry Leiber. When

Belle Harbor, 1935. From left, Mike, Dad, Joanne, Mom.

my dad saw he was going to lose our house, he built with his own hands an apartment for us in the basement of my grandfather's house next door. The thing I remember most about those living quarters is the Victrola console. Over and over and over again, even before I could read, I played the 12-inch 78 rpm RCA Red Seal recording of Richard Strauss's *Salome's Dance*. Until boogie-woogie came along, Strauss was my favorite.

When I was four, the family moved to Sunnyside, Queens, where we lived until I was sixteen. The tension in our household was pronounced. An engineer without a degree working as a draftsman, Dad held two eight-hour jobs. He'd awaken at 5:00 a.m. and sometimes be gone till 2:00 A.M. He was a talented man who dealt with an abundance of anger. Mom could be the sweetest of women, nurturing and attentive. During those times when her depression led to hospitalization, though, Dad hired a woman to care for us. My sister and I naturally resented her, and a close bond was forged between us. If the caretaker were to scold either of us, she'd have to deal with both of us. When Mom came home, we were overjoyed. The sun came out and WQXR, the classical station, played continually. I grew up on Strauss, Shostakovich, and Sibelius.

Music was a metaphor for my mother's family's superior attitude. They patronized my dad, who, despite his intelligence, had no such cultural background. My own attraction to music, however, had nothing to do with social hierarchies. It was purely visceral. And as much as I loved symphonies and tone poems, it was black music that excited my deepest passion. I heard the lyricism in Richard Strauss, I felt the elegance of Bach, but boogie-woogie really reached my eight-year-old soul.

Leiber

Red-hot songs were born on the black streets of Baltimore where I delivered five-gallon cans of kerosene and ten-pound bags of soft coal.

The first record I remember was "Boogie Express" by Derek Sampson; the second was a collection of folk blues by Josh White that included "Outskirts of Town."

Jerry with mother, Manya, in the middle,
relatives on either side, Baltimore, 1941.

I was an errand boy for my mom and the only white boy that delivered to the black families in the neighborhood. They liked me because I brought the light. I became part of their families. Inside those households, radios were always playing. Music was everywhere. Music was running through my head and coursing through my veins. My heart was flooded with boogie-woogie.

When Mom sent me on those errands, I dutifully obeyed. Manya Lerner Leiber was no one to mess with. She was a short, stocky woman known for heaving a six-foot Okie through the plate glass window of her grocery store. The man had made the mistake of growing impatient. After a few minutes in line, he said, "What the fuck do I have to do to get a pint of ice cream around here?" I remember my mother grabbing his belt buckle with one hand and his shirt collar with the other. The next thing I knew, he was on the sidewalk, flat on his back, covered with shattered glass.

Dad's death, due to a cerebral hemorrhage, was traumatic for all of us—Mom, me, and my two older sisters. He died on my fifth birthday. I adored the man. Every night he would come home with a toy or a box of strawberries for me. He had several skills. He was a whiz at numbers. In fact, he did the income taxes for his milk customers, who were, for the most part, illiterate. Many years later I learned that he had taught Hebrew and had written music for a synagogue in the small Polish town where he and my mom had met and married.

Five is much too young for a kid to encounter death. Dad's death scared the living daylights out of me. At the funeral I leaned over the grave just as his casket was lowered. When the earth, wet from an early shower, gave way, I slipped and began falling. At the last moment, my uncle Nat grabbed my arm. I remember swinging above the grave, staring at the dark hole in the ground. You could call this the defining scene of my childhood.

Stoller

Two sets of memories sit side by side in the book of my New York childhood.

The first set swings between happy and unhappy. My mother is demonstrative in her love for my sister and me. Sometimes, in a lovely voice, she'll sing a Gershwin tune or a song by Irving Berlin. At other times her voice is filled with sadness. She's a beautiful woman who I see withdrawing from the world. My dad withdraws into his work. So in different ways, and at different times, they both seem to disappear. As a result, I feel alone.

The second set of memories, though, is joyful. The second set is musical. Not only have I discovered a place where I too can withdraw, I've found a friend. His name is Al Levitt and I meet him at camp. His life is more unconventional than mine. He lives with his father in the

Wo-chi-ca summer camp, 1943.
From left, Mike and Joanne.

heart of Manhattan. His mother is far sicker than mine; paralyzed, she's restricted to a hospital in the Bronx. Al and his father seem to live a free lifestyle on the Upper West Side. If I spend the weekend there, we might go out for breakfast at Nedick's. The idea of a hot dog for breakfast is startling and exciting. It's a jazz breakfast.

It's a jazz world that Al and I discover. First, it's Louis Armstrong and His Hot Five; then it's Jelly Roll Morton and Baby Dodds; then it's rolling, rollicking pianists like Fats Waller. But it's still boogie-woogie that's moving me most.

Starting at age five, I have lessons with my aunt, the concert pianist. That isn't fun. She's old school. That means if my fingers aren't properly curved, she slaps my hand—hard. After a certain point, aunt or no aunt, I quit. Next up is Louis Kanterovsky, an itinerant piano teacher who works our neighborhood door to door. Nice gentleman, but also old school. Old school isn't working for me.

Then, by chance, someone in our neighborhood hears me playing boogie-woogie and mentions to my mother that he knows James P. Johnson, the great stride and boogie-woogie pianist. "Would young Michael be interested in lessons?" asks the neighbor.

The idea sends me soaring. The next day I'm on a subway to Jamaica, Queens, to meet the man.

Leiber

My Baltimore neighborhood was mostly Polish and Italian. Jews and blacks were disposable. I joined up with a street gang. We tried breaking into a couple of houses and failed miserably. Kelly, Rookie, Lefty, and Amigo—my partners in crime—were would-be tough guys. I wasn't the toughest guy in the gang, but after my buddy Dunbar taught me the left hook, I was the best boxer. I was also strong from dragging thirty-pound sacks of potatoes and onions up from the basement of my mom's store, where she sold everything from pork chops to Kotex.

Dunbar was four years older than me. He was my man. He liked me because I brought kerosene and coal from my mother's store to his mother's house. I liked him because he invited me up to his roof and showed me his pigeons. He allowed me to pet the babies. Dunbar loved his pigeons. I watched him feed them and looked longingly as he took a deep drag on his Old Gold. Dunbar was cool.

My first language was Yiddish. In fact, during my first day of school in kindergarten when the teacher was testing our alertness, I seemed to be the quickest. "What is this object?" she asked, holding up a salad fork. "A *gopl*," I answered, using the correct Yiddish term. My classmates howled. I died.

By the time I was ten, Mom saw her Jerome as a contender for the electric chair. She worried about my delinquent ways and made sure that my appearance pointed me in a different direction. She dressed me in camel hair coats and fine cotton shirts. I liked the look and would soon tolerate nothing but hand-sewn British loafers.

If I were to be reinvented in my mom's eyes, I would become my father—but with a law degree and a Savile Row suit. In fact, when I started smoking Old Gold cigarettes at the age of nine, my mother said with great pride, "Look at him, he smokes just like a man; he smokes like his father."

I got into some big fights. The most damaging one occurred on a rainy afternoon in front of my mother's store. A small gang of neighborhood toughs had gathered in front of the store and started chanting, "Jewboy, get that Jewboy!" I looked around and caught sight of two cops leaning against the hood of their patrol car, smiling with their arms crossed in front of their chests. They were watching—waiting for me to get the shit beat out of me. As I tried to gain entrance to my mother's store, one of the bullies pushed me. My

Jerry, age 11, Baltimore.

Hebrew books went sliding across the slick wet street. One does not allow these holy books to touch the ground, and I was horrified at the idea that I would go to hell for this terrible transgression. I started running to rescue my books and was pushed a number of times. I got so angry I started throwing punches. One assailant was someone I knew. I realized I could beat him and started going at him the way Dunbar had taught me.

Part of the crowd was screaming, "Jewboy! Jewboy! Get that

Jew!" while others were silent. But the battle had barely begun when my mother showed up and whisked me away. As she marched me into the candy store, she smacked me across the face. "Fighting again, Jerome? Fighting again?" She smacked me again. It hurt like hell. "You gonna end up in the 'lectric chair."

Stoller   When I reached the home of James P. Johnson in Jamaica, I didn't know what to expect. In my mind, it was as if Beethoven were about to give me a lesson—except that, unlike James P. Johnson, Beethoven had never given a piano lesson to Fats Waller.

Mrs. Johnson greeted me at the door. Her hair was snow-white. She was the first black person I'd ever seen with white hair. I was nervous when Mr. Johnson himself strolled into the room. He introduced himself politely and invited me to sit next to him at the piano bench. I feared severity. If my aunt was any indication of how a master instructs a disciple, I was in for it. My attempts at boogie-woogie, with its formidable technical challenges, were sincere but hardly stellar. I needed help.

Fortunately for me, James P. Johnson was a gentle man. He sensed my awkwardness and put me at ease. He explained the fundamentals, not in theory but in practice. To make it easy for me, he demonstrated everything in the key of C. He played the bass line slowly enough so I could see what he was doing. Then he repeated the pattern, over and again. He explained the twelve-bar structure.

"Understanding structure," he said, "is the key to confidence."

My confidence grew as the lessons continued. It didn't matter that the trip to his house required long rides on both subway and bus. James P. Johnson was, after all, showing me how to make the sounds that I'd always wanted to make.

The lessons went on for a few months. I remember our last time together. On that day I was aware of the fact that I might never see him again. I noticed the light streaming through the living room curtains. I also noticed the bottle of Southern Comfort that always sat atop his grand piano. He took a nip as he watched me play. When I was through, Mr. Johnson was too kind to point out my flaws. Instead, he was encouraging. He knew not to break my spirit.

"Keep at it," he said, "and someday you'll make a living banging those keys."

Later I'd learn that James P. Johnson was not only Fats Waller's mentor, but a phenomenal composer and *the* preeminent stride pianist. At the time, though, he did well to give a kid from Sunnyside a strong taste for the blues.

West Coast Convergence

Leiber Mom was sharp. She sold the small grocery store and bought a larger place, a notions store that sold pots and pans and everything in between. After that operation took off, she sold it as well. That's when she decided that the two of us would move to Los Angeles. My sisters were living in California, and Mom wanted to be closer to them. One was enrolled at the University of California at Berkeley in the political science department, and the other was married to a chief petty officer in the navy.

My twelve-year-old soul caught fire just thinking about the adventure. In my imagination, I'd be living in the land of the radio shows. *The Green Hornet, The Shadow, Gang Busters, Amos 'n' Andy*, and a host of dramas carried me through my world of make-believe. It was hard to believe that we were going to Los Angeles, but when Manya made up her mind, that was it.

The next thing I knew, we were on a Greyhound bus heading west. It was late summer and the ride was endless. The ride was also mortifying. When Manya decided to change her corset, she and I would go to the last seat in the back of the bus and, amidst a chorus of grunts and groans, I held up a sheet to ensure her privacy.

Manya persevered, schlepping me and her corset behind her. We rolled across the wheat fields of America. We tooled through Missouri. In Oklahoma I was busy looking for cowboys. I was convinced two teenaged girls were looking at me and giggling. I checked to see if my fly was open and it wasn't. The girls were just flirting. We exchanged smiles. Their giggles sounded like familiar songs. I dreamed all night.

In New Mexico, a Native American sold me a pair of turquoise earrings for a buck seventy-five and asked me where I was going.

"LA," I said.

He smiled and said, "Be careful. People who go to California fall asleep."

That night, gazing at a full moon over Arizona, I couldn't sleep.

Morning in California. Greyhound pressing on. The desert, the sun, the bus fumes, the grilled cheese sandwich at the truck stop in Riverside. Pomona, West Covina, the first sign that says Los Angeles, the first palm tree, ads for bungalows in Beverly Hills, Burma Shave, Chesterfields, Lucky Strikes, Dorothy Lamour on a billboard.

My eyes are popping, my heart is pounding: I'm in Hollywood. Hollywood and Vine! The streets are crowded with people cheering. What's happening? Could they be celebrating the arrival of Manya and Jerome Leiber?

"The sheets, Jerome, the sheets," says Mom. "Hold up the sheets, I gotta change."

By this time, all the other passengers have gotten off.

"Hurry up," the bus driver yells back to me and Mom.

"What's all the noise about out there?" Manya asks me.

"I don't know," I say.

"Go find out," she orders.

A brass band is playing "Columbia, the Gem of the Ocean" while marching down Vine Street. Confetti is falling from the tops of buildings.

I ask the bus driver what the noise is all about. He looks at me in disbelief. "Sonny, the war is over. World War II is over."

I tell Mom the war is over.

"Oh," she says.

Stoller   In our household there was talk of moving out west. My father saw business potential in California, but it didn't happen overnight. Meanwhile, I was burning up the subway track from Queens to the city. I couldn't stay away from the city. I was fixated on Fifty-second Street. My pal Al and I came alive on that street. That's where we grew up.

Once I got to Manhattan, Al and I would run over to Columbus Circle and groove on the soapbox speakers. Their rhetorical cadences were like jazz riffs. The most exciting jazz riffs, though, emanated from the newfangled style called bebop. Al and I had progressed through the traditional New Orleans style. We'd gone deep into boogie-woogie and come out the other end. We loved Fats Waller and Count Basie and modern mainstreamers like Coleman Hawkins and Lester Young. We marveled at Erroll Garner, a magician at the keyboard. But most exciting of all was the scene at the Three Deuces, one of the main Fifty-second Street clubs, where Charlie "Yardbird" Parker was in charge. Bird was the resident genius of Fifty-second Street. His harmonic sense was amazing. He played at tempos that left me breathless.

The Three Deuces was a club so tiny that Miles Davis had to stand in the passageway next to the stage. There was Max Roach, the drummer, an inch away from my elbow. There was Curly Russell, plucking his bass practically under my nose. It was heaven.

Pianists Thelonious Monk and Tadd Dameron at the Royal Roost; trumpeter Fats Navarro; fat-toned tenor players like Lucky Thompson, Stan Getz, and Brew Moore; the great singers, Billie Holiday, Ella Fitzgerald, and Sarah Vaughan, who was recording with Dizzy Gillespie. I caught them all. I had their records, I had their ideas running through my head. Their music kept me up at night.

On Saturday afternoons Al and I would put on our navy peacoats and run up to Harlem, where, through one of our camp counselors, we had joined a private social club on 124th Street. Upstairs the club had pool tables; downstairs they ran jam sessions with a slew of young cats looking to sound like Bird. The club was about everything hot and everything cool. The jukebox featured less adventuresome but equally satisfying stuff like Lonnie Johnson's "Tomorrow Night," Bull Moose Jackson's "I Love You, Yes I Do," and Paul Williams's "Hucklebuck."

It was the late forties, and Harlem was the right place at the right time.

Leiber
I loved California. The palm trees, the movie stars. I didn't see one movie star, but I knew they were there.

Mom and I found a bungalow in the middle of LA. Wasn't much, but it was home. In school I was taken on a tour of historic homes in Pasadena, and I fell passionately in love with the Gamble House designed by the famous firm of Greene and Greene. I didn't know I was looking at the supreme example of the turn-of-the-century Craftsman movement. All I knew was that the flow of shingles and wood was poetry to my eyes. One day, I swore, if the gods blessed me with good fortune, this would be my house.

You dream big in California.

That dream was interrupted by a religious obligation—my bar mitzvah. Mom thought it fitting that we have the service back in Baltimore with all my relatives. For a while, then, we relocated to our home city. But neither my mother nor I was happy there. California kept calling. And, just like that, we found ourselves returning to LA. Our neighborhood, Larchmont, was close to the famous gates that guard Paramount Studios.

Once I saw a man in a pinstripe suit and fedora hat approaching the gates. He was looking up at the sky and mouthing words.

"Is that man nuts?" I asked one of the gate guards for whom I fetched cigarettes.

"You should be so nuts, kid. That's Irving Berlin, the greatest songwriter in the world."

"Can I tell him hello?"

"Just make it short. He's busy writing a song."

I went up to him and said, "Mr. Berlin, may I shake your hand?"

"Sure, put it there, pal."

Later that week, the same guard let me through the gates so I could find the offices of the director Cecil B. DeMille. As luck would have it, the door was open and a strikingly beautiful woman sat in the reception room behind an art deco desk. As she stood up to greet me, I saw that her figure was as alluring as her face.

"What can I do for you, young man?"

"I'd like to speak to Mr. DeMille."

"Concerning what?"

"I want to be in pictures. I want to tap-dance and play drums."

"I'm afraid he's busy now. But if you return later in the week, perhaps he'll have a minute to spare."

I returned the next day. Surprisingly, the secretary smiled. She liked me. I liked her. Mr. DeMille didn't have time to see me, but I did have time to run down to the commissary and bring the secretary a little ice cream.

The same thing happened the following day and the day after that. After I did whatever favors the secretary required, she allowed me to sit in the office and read *Modern Screen* and *Daily Variety*.

Then one day it happened.

She looked up and said, "Mr. DeMille will see you."

I was completely unprepared. I was so hooked into the routine of running errands, reading trade papers in the reception room, and sneaking peeks at the secretary's gorgeous gams that I had dismissed the possibility of actually meeting DeMille.

I freaked out and couldn't move off the couch.

The smiling secretary helped me up and escorted me into the great man's office.

There he was, seated behind a massive desk, looking like a European general who had conquered half the world.

He was all business. "What can I do for you?"

I spit out my words. "I'm an actor, a tap dancer, and a drummer."

"Those are a number of talents all in one person. Can you tell me where you studied drumming?"

"A friend."

"Can you tell me where you learned acting?"

"I taught myself."

"Very good. Well, my time is limited, so let me give you some candid advice."

"I would appreciate that, sir."

"Learn gymnastics," said DeMille. "Learn fencing and body building. If it turns out you can't act, at least you'll be strong and attractive."

Welcome to the Golden Age of Hollywood.

If you lived in LA in the forties, even if you were a teenager from

Maryland, you were touched by high drama. Or low drama. Or some kind of drama.

Theater, along with Greco-Roman wrestling, attracted me. As a junior high school student, I ran track as well. But it was drama that I wanted most.

In a dream I kept hearing the song "Wrapped Up in a Dream." The dream was all blue—sky blue California meeting the black blue of some sexy singer moaning low.

I was happy to be working summers at the Circle Theater where I swept the floors and saw patrons to their seats. That's where I met Syd Chaplin—Charlie's son—and an actress named Diana Dill, who would soon marry Kirk Douglas. It was exciting stuff. I was enthralled with all things theatrical. Chaplin said I had "dramatic flair." That's all I needed to hear. "But be patient," he said. "Eventually we'll cast you in something that's right for you."

It never happened. By then I was sixteen—and an impatient sixteen at that. I'd been sweeping the floor of the theater and tearing tickets for nearly two years. And when a kid barely a year older than me, and a lousy actor to boot, was chosen over me in a play about Sherlock Holmes, I was heartbroken.

"I'm terribly sorry, Jer," Chaplin said, "but the kid's someone's nephew. There's nothing I can do about it. Be patient, something good will come along, sooner or later."

The injustice was too much for my young sensibility, and I quit. Suddenly I was rudderless. All the energy I had put into the Circle Theater and its cozy community was yielding nothing. I was jumping out of my skin with frustration when I came across an ad in the local *Larchmont News* saying "Wanted: Busboy. 8pm to 4am. Must be 18 or over." My face lit up. I could pretend to be eighteen. That's a job I could do.

Stoller

We moved to LA when I was sixteen. We lived on the edge of downtown, and I was not at all unhappy. Back in New York, when we were still in Sunnyside, my parents used a phony address to get me into Forest Hills High School. They saw Forest Hills as a step up from our lower middle-class status. I saw it as a step down because, unlike summer camp, it was virtually all white. The kids had money, some even had cars. Only a few were into music. For the most part, I felt alienated and bored. I created something of a scandal by escorting a black girl to the junior prom. In 1948, Forest Hills wasn't ready for interracial dating. I was. Al Levitt and I had also dated Puerto Rican girls and thought nothing of it. Discrimination was intolerable, especially when it came to members of the opposite sex.

Dad moved us to California because of what he considered a sure-thing opportunity. By then Joanne was Phi Beta Kappa at the University of Michigan and dating my future brother-in-law, Fred Dykstra. Mom didn't want to leave New York, but my father insisted. He was to become his boss's partner in a West Coast branch of their firm. He'd been working for a company that designed, manufactured, and installed counterweight systems for theatrical curtains. They each put up $5,000 to kick it off. To do the designing and manufacturing, Dad put on overalls in the morning; then to do the selling, he put on a suit and tie in the afternoon. The business did well. Ironically, though, his former boss used a legal loophole to fire Dad. As a result, in his late forties, Dad had to start over from scratch. Meanwhile, my mother, lost in a strange city, suffered several severe bouts of depression.

I liked Belmont High, the school just outside downtown. Half the kids were Mexicans. Then there were Chinese and Japanese kids, black kids, and kids from the South Sea Islands. All the hipsters back in New York warned me that LA was really square, but they were wrong.

Mike, front row, third from right, Los Angeles, 1950.
With the Counts, a social club.

It was in Belmont High School in typing class. I thought she was really pretty. She was Filipino. Her name was Elizabeth, but everyone called her China (pronounced Cheena). I guess she liked me too, and we started hanging out together, walking to Tommy's at Rampart and Beverly for chiliburgers after school, going to movies and school dances. Her crowd was mostly Chicano; they dressed in the Pachuco style. I adopted the style and started sporting chino pants, heavy-soled cordovan shoes, and Hawaiian or dark gabardine shirts. I learned to talk the talk—at least a few phrases—and walk the walk. The only thing I couldn't do was wear my hair in a "duck's ass" because it was too curly.

The more China and I saw each other, the more intimate we became. Sometimes we would sit together on her bed under a blanket made into a tent while she burned some powder in a small tin. It smelled like pot, but it was only a remedy for her asthma.

Eventually she became my first sexual experience. Once we started, it was hard to stop. The first time it was in her bedroom when her folks were out. Then it was in my car, in the alleyway next to her house, in the deserted balcony of the movie theater, in the little electric boats on the lake in Echo Park. We must have had sex five or six times a week for a couple of years. We tried to be careful—whatever that meant—but I never used a condom. I just guessed she couldn't, thank God, get pregnant.

Years later, after I had left LA, I came back to see my father and called China's old number from a phone booth. A girl I remembered from high school answered. She had married China's brother.

"I remember you," she said. "Are you still playing the piano?"

"A little bit," I said.

Then I asked about China.

"Oh, she got married to some guy and moved to the Philippines. She had five kids, but then she died from an asthma attack."

I got an empty feeling in my gut.

Leiber   The all-night scene at Clifton's Cafeteria in downtown LA was something out of Edward Hopper. Lonely ladies sipping tea at corner tables. Old men comforting themselves with the fifty-cent corned beef and cabbage special. Hookers and their johns warming up on post-tryst bowls of chili.

It was a bitch of a gig for me—the graveyard shift. In addition to my washing duties, I was lugging heavy trays and platters from the dining room to the kitchen, where I stacked them into a two-ton stainless steel dishwasher. I worked some winter nights, but mainly I put in my time during summers when the weather was hot and humid.

Time weighed on my mind. The scene got stale, the food got worse, but I hung around. I needed the money to purchase the brown suede shoes befitting a young man of my distinction.

Then one night it happened: I was carrying a tray of dirty dishes back to the kitchen when I passed through an alcove where the short-order cook was resting his head on the palm of his hand. He was leaning on the lower portion of a Dutch door. A joint was resting in his mouth, the sweet smoke of marijuana lazily caressing his face. His eyes were half-closed as he drifted off to the music coming from the kitchen radio. Hunter Hancock, the rhythm-&-blues-loving disc jockey, had a show called *Harlem Hit Parade*. He was playing Jimmy Witherspoon's "Ain't Nobody's Business."

I can't explain my reaction, but at that very moment I was transported into a realm of mystical understanding. The light came on. Witherspoon turned on the light. Maybe it was the power and absolute confidence of his voice. Maybe it was the lyrics. I don't know.

> *If I should take a notion*
> *To jump into the ocean*
> *It ain't nobody's business if I do*

Whatever it was, I was never the same again. Whatever Witherspoon was doing, I could do. Whatever Witherspoon was saying, I could say. The doors had opened. I had entered his world.

Stoller

Music was the world that intrigued me, but I wasn't sure of the way in. I wasn't sure of anything. As the forties turned into the fifties, uncertain times were upon us.

My mother's brother, Guy Endore, a successful novelist and screenwriter, was blacklisted. In February 1950, Senator Joseph McCarthy kicked off his campaign of career-busting, life-destroying smears with the words, "I have here in my hand a list of two hundred and five people that were known to the Secretary of State as being members of the Communist Party and who are nevertheless still working and shaping policy in the State Department." The accusations soon spread to Hollywood and, before we knew it, FBI agents were

Mike, Los Angeles, 1950. Note framed picture of George Gershwin.

at our door, questioning my mother about her brother's "subversive" activities. Mom was distraught. Uncle Guy's film career suffered greatly. Later, however, he published a best-selling novel, *The King of Paris*.

I escaped the depressive atmosphere at home by sometimes playing piano in a group led by the Vasquez brothers, guys I met at Belmont High. We had a gig at a dance at the Alexandria Hotel where our sit-in trumpeter, a movie-star-handsome guy with a seductive Miles Davis–like tone, was Chet Baker. We became friendly. I couldn't help but be impressed when he told me he'd played with Charlie Parker during Bird's club appearances in LA. I told Chet I'd been writing a few bebop tunes, and he said he'd like to hear them.

I had fun playing with the Vasquez brothers and Chet, but I knew I lacked the chops to be a really good jazz pianist. I guess I had some talent, but practicality told me my talent might be best expressed in composition. That realization led me to start studying with Arthur Lange, known as the Dean of Hollywood orchestrators. Lange had scored many movies. Maybe that was a skill I could learn.

But because Dad was not getting rich and Mom was not getting better, I had to work. Work meant pocket money. I like to say that Sammy Davis, Jr. and I worked together. He was on stage at the Million Dollar Theater while I walked up and down the aisles hawking ice cream. I also worked as an usher and doorman at the Orpheum, another downtown movie palace. I can't tell you how many times I saw *Father of the Bride*. I had that miserable script memorized. It was a boring job—so boring, in fact, that when business was slow, I'd doodle in a notebook. One day the manager, looking at my abstract doodle, asked me in a friendly manner, "What's that you're drawing?"

"The sex act," I told him.

He looked horrified. "You're fired," he said.

Leiber
I was at Fairfax High School in the middle of Jewish LA. I was a bit of a dandy, a bit of a hipster, a bit of this, and a bit of that, but chiefly, after my Witherspoon epiphany, an impassioned would-be songwriter. That's what led me to my part-time job at Norty's, a little record shop that catered to old Jews and hipsters like me on Fairfax Avenue directly across from Canter's Delicatessen. They sold Frankie Laine records—not to mention Mickey Katz's version of "Mule Train"—as well as cantorials from Russia and Poland.

Norty Beckman, who owned Norty's, hired me as a shipping clerk and sometime salesman. I worked there to be closer to music, but the music of the day was "If I Knew You Were Comin', I'd've Baked a Cake" and "How Much Is That Doggie in the Window?" Both records drove me crazy. I stuck my fingers in my ears to get away from the crap.

One morning, though, my ears opened. A sharp-dressed man came into the store and whipped out his card. "Lester Sill, National Sales Manager, Modern Records." I was impressed. Modern was a hip little label specializing in the blues artists I loved. Right off the bat, Sill started pitching me new records, as if I had any power to buy anything. I tried to explain that I was nobody, but he kept talking. He said, "Kid, I think you're gonna like this music." And, man, was he right! I loved the music because the music was the stuff I'd heard in Baltimore and in LA on Hunter Hancock's radio show. The stuff was John Lee Hooker singing "Boogie Chillen'." Suddenly the epiphany re-exploded, expanded, and knocked me on my ass.

Lester Sill brought in this new epiphany. He embodied it. He was wearing a tan double-breasted suit with a subtle powder-blue pinstripe. His suit impressed me mightily. But "Boogie Chillen'" impressed me even more. John Lee Hooker delineated his raw blues while Sill did a little jig. The dance, in the style of Sandman Sims, added to my enchantment.

When the dance was done, Sill asked, "What are you going to be when you grow up, kid?"

"I'm already grown up."

"What are you going to be when you get bigger?"

"A songwriter."

"Have you written songs?"

"Sure."

"Sing me one."

"Now? Here?"

"Now," Sill insisted.

"Norty's in the back. He'll fire me."

"Don't worry about Norty. He's my buddy. Sing your song."

I sang him a few lines from "Real Ugly Woman." He cocked his head and said, "Not bad. Have any others?"

"Sure."

"Get me copies."

"How do I do that?" I asked.

"You gotta write out a lead sheet for me," he said.

"What's a lead sheet?"

"Piece of music paper with notes written on it and lyrics written under the notes."

"I don't write notes."

"Well, find someone who does."

The search was on.

Stoller I was into all kinds of music. Arthur Lange was teaching me to write for a symphony orchestra. The Vasquez brothers were teaching me rancheros. And my growing record collection, replete with Lennie Tristano and Lee Konitz, continued to floor me with the artistic intricacies of advanced bebop.

As far as work went, I took whatever I could. I was dependent on any gig I could dig up. I graduated high school in January of 1950 and started Los Angeles City College.

Though I was at best a fair piano player, I was hired by a variety of bands to play school dances and anything that paid a few dollars. Like most teenagers, I was shooting off in six different directions at once.

I wrote an ambitious piece that, two years after I composed it, was played by the Santa Monica Symphony Orchestra. Then nineteen, I invited an attractive UCLA graduate student to go to the performance with me, convinced she'd be impressed. The orchestra played it beautifully, but afterward the conductor said, "This was written by Michael Stoller, who's only seventeen." I tried to explain the age discrepancy to my date, but it was too late. The romance was aborted and my heart broken.

Leiber

An uncontrollable compulsion was driving me. I had to find a writing partner. I needed someone who could write notes down on paper. For a while I had a partner, a part-time drummer by the name of Jerry Horowitz, who gave me percussion lessons. We wrote some songs, but nothing came of it. One day he missed a writing session. I didn't hear from him for about a week. When he finally showed up, he said, "Sorry, Jer, but I can't write with you anymore. My father died and I gotta find a day job to help pay my family's bills." I was crushed. What could I say? He had lost his dad. I knew what that was all about. Before he left, though, he fished a piece of paper out of his breast pocket and said, "By the way, I played a gig last weekend in East LA and I thought the piano player was pretty good."

"You got his name?"

"Yeah. Mike Stoller."

Stoller   The call came out of the blue.

"Hi, my name is Jerome Leiber. Are you Mike Stoller?"

"Yup."

"Did you play a dance in East LA last week?"

"Yup."

"Can you write music?"

"Yup."

"Can you write notes on music paper?"

"Yup."

"Would you like to write songs with me?"

"Nope."

"How come?"

"I don't like songs," I said.

"What do you like?"

Somewhat pretentiously, I answered, "I like Béla Bartók and Thelonious Monk."

"Anyway, I think we should meet to talk about it."

"Hey," I said, "if you want to come over, come over."

It seemed to me that the doorbell rang as I hung up the phone.

Leiber
I was in a big hurry. I was racing to get a lead sheet made on the song I was going to submit to Lester Sill. The muse was pushing me. Pushing hard. I didn't know this Stoller character from a hole in the wall, but if Horowitz said he was cool, he was cool.

I ran over to his house. The door opened, and I saw a kid my age with a beret on his head and a Dizzy Gillespie–type goatee on the end of his chin. *A bebopper*, I thought to myself. *Oh, shit. Not one of them.*

I had a notebook filled with lyrics.

"Like I told you on the phone, I want to write songs," I said.

Mike just stood there staring at me until his mother called from the kitchen, "Aren't you going to invite your friend in?"

Stoller
The first thing I noticed about Jerry was the color of his eyes. One was blue and one was brown. I'd never seen that before. There was something intriguing about it, but it was strange—almost as strange as his request that we write songs together.

The only songs that really interested me were bebop compositions. I had the impression that Jerry probably wanted to write the kind of tunes you heard on the radio—moon, June, and all that. I couldn't have cared less.

But I figured if he'd taken the trouble to come to my house, I might as well look at the speckled composition book he was holding. The things that caught my attention—the things that really changed my life—were the ditto marks.

Jerry had written a line like, "She's a real ugly woman, don't see how she got that way."

The second line was merely dittos, indicating a repetition of the first line.

The third line read, "Every time she comes 'round, she runs all my friends away."

It wasn't simply that the lyrics were witty. It was more than that.

"These are blues!" I said. "You didn't tell me you were writing blues. I love the blues."

It was May, and I had a summer job lined up.

"We can start in the fall," I said.

"I want to start now."

"I can't. I gotta wait."

"I don't wanna wait."

"Well, you'll have to if you want me to write with you."

"I want to write with you," Jerry said, "but I hate waiting."

"Okay," I said, walking over to the piano. I started playing some blues. Jerry improvised some lyrics and sang them as if he had been born in Mississippi.

We shook hands and said, "We'll be partners." And so began a six-decade argument with no resolution in sight. It was 1950. We were seventeen.

Leiber

From the get-go, our energies were different. Mike was cautious and I was impetuous. You might even say I was reckless. The Jimmy Witherspoon epiphany at Clifton's Cafeteria was the light leading me forward. I knew I could write; I *had* to write. I tried to convince Mike that we had to get started before the summer ended. Then came a stroke of good luck. Mike was fired from his job at the Orpheum Theater. It was only July, and so we got started.

The sessions took place over at Mike's house because he had an upright piano. On the wall over the piano was a photo of George Gershwin autographed to Mike's mom. Our method was simple—

Mike sat at the piano and started fooling around, and I'd throw out ideas—lyrics, titles.

Stoller

Jerry was an idea machine. The ideas just kept coming. For every situation, Jerry had at least twenty ideas. There was no doubt that the kid was brilliant and absolutely tireless. The fact that he acted out his ideas—sang them, even danced to them—took the tedium out of writing. We wanted to have fun, although our notion of fun was rooted in authenticity. As would-be songwriters, our interest was in black music and black music only. We wanted to write songs for black voices. When Jerry sang, he sounded black, so that gave us an advantage. And it didn't hurt that James P. Johnson had given me a few lessons.

Leiber

Mike was a hipster. He was quiet, and his cool depended on maintaining a certain reserve. I respected that. If I brought heat and he brought cool, I saw that as a good combination. Besides, I loved his playing. He had a remarkable memory and could recreate almost anything he had ever heard. As a musician, he had a fluency and familiarity with a wide variety of styles. When he started to noodle, I could see that he had a large musical vocabulary.

Stoller

Jerry's verbal vocabulary was all over the place— black, Jewish, theatrical, comical. He could paint pictures with words, and the words contained all sorts of colors, textures, and tones. Not only that, he was fast.

Leiber If Mike had clung to his bebop bias, that might have been a problem. But the blues broke him down and the blues freed him up. For all his love of that high-minded technically complex jazz, Mike's heart was in the blues. He was as passionate about blues as I was. Blues was the bottom line. The blues was our bond—from that day forward. The blues became the basis of a lifetime of work.

Stoller Bebop is a serious music, a beautiful music, and although I would never be a great bop pianist, that was the form that I considered the highest art. At the same time, I recognized that, for all its complexity, the foundation of bop—in fact, the foundation of all jazz—is the blues. At first, writing a three-minute blues seemed like a simple task. But I saw that blues composition had its subtleties, and, as Jerry and I started working together, those subtleties interested me more and more.

So I would sit there and start to riff, and Jerry would start singing a line, and sometimes the line matched the notes I was playing, and sometimes the line didn't. Sometimes he'd want me to change the music to match the words, and sometimes I'd want him to change the words to match the music. Often we'd fight. Fighting was part of the creative process. Jerry was as stubborn as me. Or maybe it's better to say that he was as attached to his words as I was to my music. We often heard things differently. But after pushing and pulling, we'd usually wind up with something that surprised and delighted us both: a good song.

Leiber

It didn't take long for us to build up a small inventory. Our point man, of course, was Lester Sill, our only link to the real world of the record business. That world was especially interesting at the start of the fifties. As Lester explained it, the major record labels had little interest in what they considered heavily ethnic music. Sure, Louis Armstrong was on Decca along with Ella Fitzgerald and the Mills Brothers, but the vast majority of black artists, especially the ones we considered all-the-way authentic, were on small labels like Atlantic, Modern, Aladdin, Savoy, Specialty, Swing Time, Imperial, and King.

"The big labels," explained Lester, "like RCA, Columbia, and Decca are ignoring the really great popular Negro artists 'cause they just don't understand or care about the music. They don't think it's worthwhile, artistically or commercially. Well, I don't have to tell you how wrong they are."

Like Lester, many of the label owners were Jewish. "Look at the way the big iron and steel companies threw the scraps to the Jews," said Lester. "That's how Jews started in the scrap metal business. Same thing in music. The majors see great artists like Jimmy Witherspoon as scrap. They don't want to deal with what they consider junk. Well, some of these small labels were actually junk dealers before they got into the music game. Through experience, they learned what some see as junk might actually be precious jewels."

Were Mike and I making precious jewels? Could two teenage kids pretend to understand the kind of songs that grown-up black men and women wanted to sing and hear?

Lester heard our material and said, "Yes." Then he added, "*Hell,* yes."

"I'm setting up an appointment for you to meet the Bihari brothers, the guys who own Modern. I want them to hear your stuff."

Stoller
In those days we knew nothing about demos and, even if we did, we couldn't afford to make them. If we wanted to get our song recorded, we had to play it—live—in front of the people who could make it happen. So Jerry and I went to meet the people. We jumped into my beat-up '37 Plymouth and headed for Beverly Hills.

LA was wide-open back then. There were oil wells pumping just off Wilshire Boulevard and open fields just beyond Beverly Hills. Hope was in the air. Our plan was simple: I'd play and Jerry would sing. We were hardly cocky, but we did exhibit a certain confidence. We knew our songs were good and, even more, we knew they felt authentically black. Black was our criteria for quality.

We arrived at Modern Records' office on Canon Drive precisely on time—twelve noon. The receptionist took our names and asked us to wait. We leafed through *Billboard* and *Cash Box*, seeing that Nat "King" Cole had hit big with "Mona Lisa" and Ivory Joe Hunter with "I Almost Lost My Mind." Five minutes passed. Jerry handed me the *Los Angeles Times*. I lit up a cigarette. Ten minutes passed. Jerry lit up a cigarette. 12:20. We were both fidgety. We got up and asked the receptionist if the Biharis knew we were waiting.

"They know," she said, expressionless.

"Let's split," I said to Jerry. "I don't like being stood up. These people are incredibly rude."

The long wait had eroded my confidence. I was feeling scared. We walked up the street toward Santa Monica Boulevard and suddenly saw a sign across the street. Aladdin Records.

Aladdin had great blues artists like Charles Brown and Amos Milburn. So a few minutes after we'd stormed out of Modern, we found ourselves in the office of another record company.

Another indifferent receptionist.

"Do you have an appointment?" she asked.

"No," said Jerry, "but we have hit songs."

When he said that, a black man named Maxwell Davis happened to be walking by. Davis is truly one of the unsung heroes of early rhythm & blues. B.B. King would later say Max was responsible for his best work. A big-toned tenor sax man, a great writer, a hip arranger, and a superb musical director, Davis was in demand. All the little labels wanted him in the studio. In 1950, the year we met him, he had written and produced the smash hit "Bad Bad Whiskey" for Amos Milburn.

"Okay, boys," said Maxwell, a well-dressed gentleman who got right to the point. "Let's hear what you got."

We went into a back room where they had an upright piano. My shaken confidence returned. I wasn't sure what Jerry was going to sing, but he just started and I fell in behind. I don't remember the song, but it was an uptempo blues that probably employed a sexual metaphor.

Max chuckled and said, "What else do you have?"

We played a blues ballad called "I Love You So."

"You guys know what you're doing. I want the bosses to hear you."

The Mesner brothers, Leo and Eddie, came in to hear our songs and nodded.

We walked out the door with a song contract and two big smiles.

Leiber When Lester Sill heard what happened, he took us back to Modern and this time made sure we met the Bihari brothers, who also invited their ace singing group, the Robins, to hear our stuff. We let loose with something we had just written, a different take on the Bible than what I'd studied at Hebrew school:

Well, back in the days of old King Saul
Every night was a crazy ball
The cats smoked hay through a rubber hose
And the women, they wore transparent clothes
That's what the Good Book says, boy,
That's what the Good Book says . . .

The Robins dug our new creation myth and cut "That's What the Good Book Says" a month later. It came out in early 1951. A real record. Our very first, with our names on it, although misspelled. But it was real.

Stoller We had our first record and, believe it or not, within a month we had our second.

Leiber One miracle followed another. Our second release was by Jimmy Witherspoon, the singer who got me hooked on songwriting. The tune was "Real Ugly Woman." The story begins around Christmastime 1950 at a concert at the Shrine Auditorium where promoter Gene Norman put together a Blues Jamboree with artists like Wynonie Harris, Helen Humes, and "Spoon." We'd gotten the song to Jimmy only a few weeks before. He loved it and promised to do it. The gods were smiling that night because the gig was taped. The song was released as a live single and was embraced by true blues people:

She's a real ugly woman—don't see how she got that way
* "   "   "   "   "   "*

Every time she comes 'round she runs all my friends away

Well, she's got great big teeth and they're out of line
She's 300 pounds of meat, she's my female Frankenstein

Spoon sang it like he meant it. He drained the thing dry. It was raw, funny, traditional, and original; it was everything Mike and I could have hoped for.

Stoller With a couple of real records under our belt and the confidence that they gave us, we went back to visit Maxwell Davis at Aladdin.

He led us back to an upright piano.

I played while Jerry sang a blues called "Hard Times."

I've got pains in my head, dead on my feet,
My pantry's empty, I ain't eaten for a week
Hard times, ooo I feel so bad
When I lost my baby, I lost everything I had . . .

"I like it," said Max the minute we were through. "I can hear Charles Brown singing it."

That very evening we played the song for Charles Brown. He lived in a gracious home in the West Adams area. In those days, he was considered as important as Nat "King" Cole. Charles had a beautiful personality—a tall, handsome man, stylishly dressed, with a feminine manner. After we gave him the lead sheet, he politely seated us on a red velvet couch while he went to the Baldwin to play our song. On the piano bench was an inner tube.

"Gentlemen," he said, "I know this appears strange but I've just gone through a hemorrhoid operation."

Despite his discomfort, Charles played and sang magnificently.

"This is a record," he said. "This is definitely a Charles Brown record."

Leiber   We weren't invited to the recording session, but that hardly mattered. When Maxwell played Charles Brown's version of "Hard Times" for us, we heard it as a work of high art.

Charles Brown.

Charles sang it with tremendous feeling; his piano playing was a study in sensitivity; and Max's tenor sax accompaniment was rich, deep, and discreet. To our ears, it was a masterpiece, just the kind of real-life blues that we dreamed of creating. And to think—it was actually being played on the radio and selling at John Dolphin's record shop on Central Avenue, where a disc jockey was working in the store window!

One day in 1952, Lester Sill reported the good news to us. "I've been to all my stops, all the places where they sell records—Woolworth's, Music City, the shoeshine stands, the candy stores—and everyone's playing it."

We were *in*. Wherever that was.

We wanted to be original—after all, we wanted to sell our songs—but we also wanted to respect the tradition. The greatness of the blues tradition comes out of emotional directness, for sure, but also a vast variety of content. The blues is about heartache and pain, but also unrestrained joy and unrestrained sex. As horny teenagers, we had no problem writing about sex. In fact, if we could find any metaphor for fucking we'd use it. In this same time zone—the early fifties—we wrote something called "Nosey Joe," recorded by the great Bull Moose Jackson.

> *There's a man in town all the women know*
> *He goes by the name of Nosey Joe*
> *Don't care if they're married, he takes his pick*
> *Long as they're women he's ready to stick . . .*
>
> *His big nose in their business*
> *That's Nosey Joe, the nosiest guy I know*

3

Makin' the Scene

Stoller Because all nice Jewish boys were expected to attend college, Jerry and I, at least for a while, attended Los Angeles City College on Vermont Avenue. As you can guess, our hearts weren't in our studies. Our hearts were in the music scene.

Los Angeles was a mecca of black music. The concentration of bebop was certainly not as great as in New York, where the new form was born, but Bird and Diz came through. Their Los Angeles disciples—like Dexter Gordon, Teddy Edwards, and Wardell Gray—were regular fixtures around town. Then there was the thrill of Central Avenue. What Fifty-second Street was to New York, Central Avenue was to LA. At the Club Alabam, the Dunbar Hotel, the Turban Room, or the Five-Four Ballroom, I'd see everyone from T-Bone Walker to Johnny Moore's Three Blazers. Over on Wilshire Boulevard, near the Ambassador Hotel, the Haig was happening. That's where I'd go see Gerry Mulligan, who'd formed a pianoless quartet with my former bandmate Chet Baker. One night I went in there with a composition under my arm. During the break I said to Chet, "I wrote something you guys might like."

Chet nodded approvingly and told Mulligan, drummer Chico Hamilton, and bassist Carson Smith to meet him in the kitchen. They read it down and played it beautifully. I thought it was great.

"You have a two-part construction," said Mulligan. "We only do three parts." He handed me back my music. It was, Thanks, but no thanks.

I was hurt. Maybe they really did play only three-part constructions, but I had the feeling that Mulligan preferred that *he* write all the material, no matter how many parts.

Mulligan was a principal architect of the Cool School, and here I had missed out on the chance to contribute to his groundbreaking combo. I got over my disappointment by transforming the piece into something I entitled "Suite Allegro," switching the trumpet/baritone sax parts to clarinet/bassoon and adding sections for violin and cello. Four or five years later, I scraped together enough money to record it.

Leiber

Norman Granz's Jazz at the Philharmonic was all the rage in the early fifties. In LA these jam sessions happened at the Shrine Auditorium. Everyone was playing with everyone else. The swing masters—Coleman Hawkins and Roy Eldridge—would blow with the boppers like Bird and Charles Mingus. Big Jay McNeely would fall on his knees and even on his back, raising his horn to the heavens and screaming out the kind of raunchy honking solos that marked the start of what would later be called rock and roll.

Lionel Hampton's brilliant band of this period showed off similar paradoxes, the kind that made music freaks like me and Mike especially happy. Hamp had a swing band, a bop band and, at the same time, a rocking, rolling R&B band. It was all exemplified by his big hit, "Flying Home." We liked that song so much that Mike and I wrote lyrics for it, putting words to the famous Illinois Jacquet tenor solo. Amos Milburn recorded our version. That form, matching lyrics to improvised jazz solos, was called "vocalese" and first developed by linguistical hipsters like King Pleasure and Eddie Jefferson.

We also wrote lyrics to "Bernie's Tune," an instrumental West Coast jazz anthem that Mike's pal Chet Baker had recorded with Gerry Mulligan. We were making inroads and finding ourselves welcome not only into the world of blues, but jazz as well. Our hearts were in the music, and our hearts were taking us places our minds could have never imagined.

Stoller
Gradually we were building a reputation. The Los Angeles rhythm & blues world of minor labels with major talents was small but bustling. Recording was cheap, shellac was cheap, ads in the trade journals were cheap—and product was in demand. Songs were needed, and we supplied that need.

Leiber
We had a champion in the form of Lester Sill, and Lester loved singing our praises. But we didn't have an agent or a song plugger, and we never promoted ourselves. Mike and I couldn't hustle if we had to. We didn't know how to sell ourselves. We believed in what we did, but only because we were convinced of its authenticity. If someone said to me, "Leiber, you got a good voice—*you* record the song," I'd say, "Hey, listen. We give ourselves a pass when it comes to writing. But singing? White guys can't sing the blues. I want Muddy Waters or Ray Charles to sing the blues." In fact, Ray

Charles, even before he hooked up with Atlantic Records, did cut one of our songs—"The Snow Is Falling."

The fact that we were selling songs didn't excite our ambition; it was hearing those songs sung by master singers that had us running back to Mike's little upright piano. At the same time, we inevitably ran into the characters—some shady, some legit—who hung around the edges of the business.

Harry Goodman ran his brother Benny's publishing firm. Harry was the guy who got us to put words to "Flying Home," a Benny Goodman–Lionel Hampton composition. Not only did he work Benny's tunes, but he had a publishing deal with Chess Records. That meant he needed blues songs, and we assured him that the blues was our specialty.

"You got hits?" Harry asked.

"We got hits," I answered.

He invited us over to his bungalow at Selma and Vine. Mike and I arrived, ready to knock him out with our newest tunes.

Harry dressed like the Duke of Windsor—if the Duke had had the head of a hippo. He reeked of high-priced French cologne and wore a diamond stickpin in his tie. The razor-sharp crease in his trousers could cut you and draw blood. Next to his desk was a wastebasket covered in khaki-colored leather.

"Pops," he said to me, "how many hits you got for me today?"

"Eight," I said.

"Eight's great. Go."

Mike went to the piano while I handed Harry a lyric sheet. Two notes into the song, Harry stopped us.

"It's shit," he said, then crumpled up the sheet and threw it in the leather wastebasket. "What else you got, Pops?" he asked.

I handed him another sheet, and Mike started playing another tune.

Again, he stopped us. "It's shit," he declared. Again, he crumpled up the sheet and threw it in the basket.

Same thing for songs three, four, five, six, and seven. The wastebasket was filling up fast.

Discouraged, I took the last one, number eight, crumpled it up and threw it in the wastebasket myself.

Harry got up from his chair and went to the basket. He fished out the sheet and smoothed it out on his desk before asking Mike to play the melody. Mike played the melody.

"What do you think?" I asked.

"It's shit," said Harry. "But it's the kind of shit I need."

I can't tell you the name of the song or whether it actually got recorded. All I remember is Harry Goodman's diamond stickpin and leather-covered wastebasket.

Stoller

Money wasn't pouring in; payouts on record royalties take forever, and when they finally arrive the check is usually half of what you expected.

I wasn't much of a dresser in those days. I'd write notes to myself on my chino pants and mend the holes at the knees with duct tape. On the other hand, Jerry always looked sharp. Rather than reject the fine wool slacks that irritated him, he wore flannel pajamas underneath to protect his skin. He had a keen eye for shoes. Elegant shoes were his thing.

One day we're driving down Fairfax, Jerry in his old Chevy, me following behind in my '37 Plymouth. Jerry spots an outlet shoe store and pulls over. I stop as well.

Jerry and I survey the window. He spots a pair of butter-colored British loafers. I spot a pair of alligators.

We go in and approach the proprietor, who eyes us suspiciously. He quotes the prices—the British loafers are $35, the alligators are $15, perhaps due to the warped soles and sun-faded color.

I have just enough cash for mine. Jerry is tapped out, but he has an idea.

"Do you need a second car?" Jerry asks the proprietor.

"What the hell are you talking about?"

"Well, I have another car," Jerry lied, "and I don't really need two. I'll trade you the one out there for this pair of shoes."

"Are you crazy?"

"No, I just want those shoes."

"What's wrong with your car?"

"Nothing. Here are the keys. Take it for a spin."

"Who's gonna watch the store?" he asks with ever-mounting suspicion.

"We will," I say. "Don't worry."

The proprietor takes a spin and returns in five minutes.

"Well, okay," he says, "where's the registration?"

"I'll get it to you in the next day or so."

And that's it. We slip on our new shoes and head for my car, Jerry striding comfortably and looking like a million bucks while I hobble along in my warped alligators.

A couple of weeks later, our mentor, Lester Sill, invited us to join him on a trip to the Bay Area. One evening we wound up at a little joint called the Champagne Supper Club. That's where we heard Linda Hopkins, who slayed us with her version of the Dominoes' "Have Mercy, Baby." We were so excited about her ability to belt the blues that we paid for her to come to LA to make some records. "Three-Time Loser" and "Tears of Joy" were released on Crystalette Records. They didn't do much. Linda, though, went on to a big career, including a smash run on Broadway playing Bessie Smith in the mid-seventies.

Another strong blues belter cut a Leiber and Stoller song that changed the course of our lives. But before that happened, we took a little side trip to the East Coast with Lester and his friend Ricky Jacobs, the most feared gin rummy maven on any coast.

4

Coastin'

Leiber It's 1951 and Ricky Jacobs is driving Lester Sill's
'49 Ford convertible, pedal to the metal, 80 mph all the way. Jacobs
is a super-slick card shark and Lester's old buddy from Philly. Mike
and I are in the backseat, shaking with fear because Ricky is speeding like a maniac.

"Gotta get there," is all Ricky can say. "Gotta make good time."

Gotta survive this trip, I'm thinking/praying/saying to myself.
Gotta hope there's a God up there keeping our asses alive.

The West Coast to East Coast trip is virtually nonstop. I look up
and we're in Oklahoma. I look up again and we're in Cincinnati.
Lester and Ricky never stop talking. Mike and I never stop shaking.

Stoller As we drove through Cincinnati, Lester started
talking about the most important music man in the city, Syd Nathan.
Lester told us how Nathan deserted the department store business in

the forties and found an old ice house, where he started a label. Of course, we knew about Nathan's King Records. He had big R&B hits, like Bull Moose Jackson's "I Want a Bow-Legged Woman" and Lonnie Johnson's magnificent "Tomorrow Night," one of the most beautiful blues ballads ever recorded. Nathan also employed Henry Glover, a brilliant A&R man, writer, arranger in the Maxwell Davis mode. Among his many accomplishments, Glover wrote "Drown in My Own Tears," a hit first for Sonny Thompson and then Ray Charles. Nathan's other creative ace was Ralph Bass, another pioneer record man, who would later work with James Brown.

Sill said that while Syd might be incapable of keeping a beat, he possessed business acumen. Nathan owned his own plant, where he cut, mastered, and manufactured the discs. He even had a printing press that turned out the record covers.

"Ownership is everything," Lester kept harping.

Leiber "Getting out of this goddamn car is everything," I kept saying.

When we finally got out for good it was in Philly, where Ricky Jacobs got into a twenty-four-hour card game that wiped out the local population. Jacobs was to gin rummy what Lucky Strike was to cigarettes; he toasted all his opponents. Word was, Ricky could beat the gin rummy champ of the Western world blindfolded. Jacobs had skills and secrets that gave him an aura of mystery and danger.

Meanwhile, Mike and I, after a Philly cheesesteak sandwich at Pat's, hopped a train. We were eager to get to New York. Lester had set up appointments for us to meet Henry Glover and Ralph Bass, Syd Nathan's guys, who worked in Manhattan.

"And don't forget to go by and see Bobby Shad," said Lester.

Stoller Meeting the R&B big shots impressed us, not only because they were older and far more accomplished than us, but because we could relate to their musical sensibilities. Bobby Shad, for instance, had his own label, Sittin' in with. I remembered that because in my early teens I had bought Charlie Ventura's recording of "Euphoria" on that very label.

We had breakfast with Bobby at a diner on Eleventh Avenue. He had just released a record, "Junko Partner" by James Waynes, that Jerry and I were nuts about.

Studio wizards like Shad, Henry Glover, and Ralph Bass were extremely cordial to us. They shook our hands and complimented us on a song or two of ours that they may have heard. They were kind and encouraging. I was happy to be back in my original stomping grounds and could have hung around longer.

Leiber Lester was calling from the City of Brotherly Love. He sounded dead serious.

"You and Mike run over to Penn Station right now and get on the first train to Philly. Be on the corner of Sixteenth and Pennsylvania tonight at exactly ten with suitcases in hand. Soon as you see us, jump in the car, and don't look back. We're heading to the coast."

"What happened?" I ask. "You guys rob a bank or something?"

"It isn't funny, Jerry. Ricky got into a jam. We gotta scram."

Mike and I didn't hesitate. We caught the train and were waiting on the corner when Lester and Ricky stopped to get us.

We returned the way we came—nonstop speedsters going for broke. With the top down and the sun scorching, I wound up with such a serious burn I couldn't blink my eyes. When we finally sailed into LA, I was toast.

But I was also happy to get back to work. The East Coast had inspired us. We had met with guys who actually made the kind of records we loved.

The trip lit a spark.

5

Absolute Harmony

Stoller In 1952, Ralph Bass, whom we had met in New York, moved to LA and set up the Federal subsidiary of King Records. Bass was a co-owner of Federal. He introduced us to the world of Little Esther, Little Willie Littlefield, and the great Johnny Otis. Johnny was a Greek who had assimilated himself into the heart of the LA 'hood as an important bandleader, songwriter, vibraphonist, and drummer. He also put on his own shows featuring the artists he had discovered and groomed, including Etta James and Little Esther. In a short period, Little Esther would record over a half dozen of our songs and Little Willie at least one important song that grew out of an argument.

Though the contentious nature of our songwriting was a constant, we'd be fools not to see that, as a team, we had something. But we'd be hard-pressed to tell you what that "something" was. Harmony might have come out in our songs, but our writing sessions were more a matter of push and pull. No matter, we kept plugging away, providing artists we admired with material we felt matched their styles.

Left to right: Mel Walker, Johnny Otis and Little Esther Phillips.

Style, of course, is everything in popular music. One wants to be in style, but one also wants to be a little ahead of the style. Ideally, one wants to create one's own style. I supposed that's what was on my mind when I sat down at the piano and started a new blues. Jerry was singing something about Kansas City, the city associated with Count Basie and Charlie Parker.

Jerry sang the first three lines in the normal twelve-bar blues pattern:

I'm going to Kansas City, Kansas City here I come
Going to Kansas City, Kansas City here I come
They got a crazy way of loving there and I'm gonna get me some

Gonna be standing on the corner Twelfth Street and Vine
Gonna be standing on the corner Twelfth Street and Vine
With my Kansas City baby and my bottle of Kansas City wine

The song was being written for Little Willie Littlefield, who had a deal on Federal Records. Jerry's idea was that we'd give him this geographically specific but musically traditional blues.

I saw it differently. I wanted it to have a melody that you could recognize if it were played instrumentally. "No," said Jerry. "It's inauthentic."

"The feeling is still authentic," I argued. "And that's all that matters."

Jerry argued back. "I don't want some jivey melody attached to these lyrics."

"And I don't want some ordinary blues line. I want something different."

"I disagree," said Jerry.

"You said that before."

"I'm saying it again."

"I heard you the first time," I said.

"So what are we going to do?" he asked.

"Let me ask you a simple question."

"Ask," Jerry urged.

"Who writes the music?"

"You."

"End of discussion."

The melody stayed. We taught the song to Little Willie at Maxwell Davis's house. Max did the arrangement and played tenor sax on the record. Ralph Bass changed the title from "Kansas City" to what he considered the hipper "K.C. Lovin'." Seven years later, Wilbert Harrison, who remembered the song, recorded it under its original title. It reached the top of all the charts. "Kansas City" became one of our most recorded tunes, with more than three hundred versions out there.

Leiber   I hate admitting that I was wrong about "Kansas City," but that time Mike was right on the money. Being right one time, though, didn't change the tone of our collaborations. The tug of war continued.

6

Hound Dog

Stoller One morning I got a call from Johnny Otis. He told me that Don Robey, the notorious label owner-promoter/gambling entrepreneur from Houston, had given him an assignment. Robey, the most prominent black man on the business side of R&B, owned Peacock and Ace Records. His artists included Johnny Ace and Willie Mae "Big Mama" Thornton. Big Mama needed a hit. Johnny invited us over to his garage to hear her rehearse.

When Jerry and I arrived and heard her start to sing, we looked at each other in amazement. In her combat boots and oversized overalls, she was formidable and a bit frightening. Her voice was a force of nature. Big Mama was absolutely magnificent.

"You have a song for her?" Johnny asked us during the break.

"We don't now," said Jerry, "but we will in a few minutes."

Big Mama Thornton.

Leiber   There was something monstrous about Big Mama. But I wasn't looking at her that way. I saw Big Mama as the perfect instrument for just the kind of deadly blues that Mike and I relished. So once Johnny gave us the word, we ran back to Mike's house on Norton—he was still living with his folks—and knocked out a song in a matter of minutes. It happened like lightning. We knew, as they say in the South, that this dog would hunt. "Hound Dog" had the right country-funky feel that the great lady embodied.

Just like that, we were back at Johnny's garage with a completed song. Mike started playing it on the piano, and Mama grabbed the lyric sheet out of my hands. Then she began to croon—not belt, mind you, but croon.

"Big Mama," I said with all the delicate charm at my command, "that ain't the way it goes."

The woman turned and faced me with a fury that knocked me back on my heels.

"I mean, I'm just *suggesting* how it goes," I said.

"I know how it go," she said. "It go like this," and she wagged her tongue at me.

All this was happening right in front of the band. The guys were having a ball, breaking up over Big Mama's attitude.

"Well, Big Mama," I continued, still looking for the magic words that would show this lady we'd written a raunchy blues and not a fluffy ballad, "maybe if you'd attack it with a little more—"

"Come here, boy," she said, motioning me to stand even closer to her. "I'll tell you what you can attack. Attack this . . ." she added, pointing to her crotch.

The band cracked up laughing.

In deference to her comedic triumph, Johnny, who was playing drums for this rehearsal, responded with the kind of lick loved by stand-up comics—*pa-dum-pum*. Dumbfounded, I was about to walk out, but then Johnny Otis, genius that he was, got up from the drum kit and came to my rescue.

"You sing it, Jerry," he said. "You show Big Mama how it goes."

Stoller

Big Mama liked Johnny's idea. She stood there with her arms folded, ready to laugh at the white teenager trying to sing the blues. As I played, Jerry sang the first few lines:

> *You ain't nothing but a hound dog, quit snooping 'round my door*
> *You ain't nothing but a hound dog, quit snooping 'round my door*
> *You can wag your tail, but I ain't gonna feed you no more*
>
> *You told me you was high class, but I can see through that*
> *You told me you was high class, but I can see through that*
> *And Daddy, I know, you ain't no real cool cat*

Suddenly the joke was over. Big Mama heard how Jerry was singing the thing. She heard the rough-and-tough of the song and, just as important, the implicit sexual humor. In short, she got it.

She took the lyric sheet from Jerry and ran it down herself.

Johnny started playing drums. By turning off his snare, he created a kind of tom-tom sound. Meanwhile, Pete Lewis adjusted the strings of his guitar to an old Southern tuning.

"That's it," said Johnny. "We're cutting it tomorrow."

Leiber

The session started on time. I was thinking, *Here I am at a real studio making a record of a song that me and Mike wrote when, only months ago, I was selling records at Norty's.*

I was excited, but Johnny was cool as a cucumber. He was sitting in the control booth, leaning back in a chair, waiting for the musicians to assemble and Big Mama to clear her throat.

Stoller We were worried because the drummer wasn't getting the feel that Johnny had created in rehearsal.

"Johnny," Jerry said, "can't you play drums on the record? No one can nail that groove like you."

"Who's gonna run the session?" he asked.

Silence.

"You two?" he asked. "The kids are gonna run a recording session?"

"Sure," I said. "The kids wrote it. Let the kids do it."

Johnny smiled and said, "Why not?"

Leiber That record was a masterpiece.

Big Mama didn't croon; she growled.

Johnny's groove was right on time.

Pete Lewis's guitar solo was on the money.

And although we were not credited as producers—back then, no one even used the term "producer"—we had written the song and run the session. Listening to the playback, hearing how Big Mama fulfilled our dream, we were the happiest teenagers in the United States of America. Others kids might have been flipping burgers or pumping gas and making money. We weren't making any money, but we were making records—blues records, records of the kind that we would have gladly bought and listened to over and over again, even if we hadn't written them.

Stoller

The writing and producing of "Hound Dog" was a mixed blessing. Certainly it gave us confidence. We got to see that we were capable craftsmen in and out of the studio. Our self-esteem got a much needed boost.

The exhilaration of creating something good was one thing, but the reality of the cold-blooded music business was something else. Later we learned that Johnny Otis put his name on the song as a composer and indicated to Don Robey, the label owner, that he, Johnny, had power of attorney to sign for us as well. Well, not only was Johnny *not* a writer of the song, he also didn't have the right to sign for us. When we saw what he was doing, we got an attorney and a new contract from Robey which, because we were underage, had to be signed by our mothers. Finally, the paperwork was in order and we were given an advance check for $1,200. The song hit the R&B charts, but the check bounced.

7

Spark

Stoller We had earned a few dollars with some local hits, but the biggest hit of all, Big Mama's "Hound Dog," went to #1, sold a million copies, and did nothing for our bank statements. We were getting screwed.

My dad was furious that we'd had this big hit and got screwed out of the money. He thought we should start our own label. Dad's father had recently died, leaving him a few thousand dollars. Dad was willing to put that money into a label of our own.

Lester Sill took it further. He said we should not only start a label, but a publishing company and a sales company as well. Lester was broke at the time, but called his friend Jack Levy, aka Jake the Snake, from his old Philly neighborhood, to put up $2,500. Dad provided an additional $2,500. The deal was simple—five guys (Dad, Lester, Jake, Jerry, and I) would own 20 percent each. As writer-producers, Jerry and I would get our shares for free. The label would be called Spark and the publishing company Quintet.

We were in business. We got a tiny one-room office on Crenshaw, between Olympic and Pico, in mid-city LA. We bought a small used desk, an even smaller beat-up sofa, and an old upright piano. The desk was for Lester to take orders. The sofa was for Jerry to sit on and start throwing out lyrics. The piano was for me.

Spark Records lasted for two years, 1954 and 1955. We put out some forty-four singles, both 45s and 78s, almost all of which were written and produced by Leiber and Stoller. A *Cash Box* story about the new label said, quite accurately, that we'd be "catering to the rhythm & blues market." The story went on:

"Lester Sill has taken over national sales for the firm. Two of the youngest A&R men in the business will head the new diskery. They are Mike Stoller and Jerry Leiber of 'Hound Dog' fame. A. L. Stoller was appointed general manager along with Jake Levy, East Coast representative. First releases 'Come a Little Bit Closer' b/w 'Farewell' by Willy and Ruth and 'Easyville' b/w 'The Whip' by Gil Bernal."

I had met Gil in Harmony 1 class at Los Angeles City College. In his honkin' Jazz at the Philharmonic style, Gil played great tenor sax. Willy and Ruth, who harmonized sweetly, sang the hell out of "Love Me," a song that came to center stage later in the fifties during our days and nights with Elvis Presley. We had discovered Willy and Ruth with a gospel quintet we'd heard in the Oakland area. We loved the quintet's sound and brought them to LA for a session. We called them the Honeybears and had them record "One Bad Stud" and "It's a Miracle." From that same group, we pulled Willy and Ruth to sing duets. We had other acts, like Garland the Great, who drove around town with his name emblazoned on the hood of his rusty Cadillac and the titles of his two Spark singles painted on the doors.

On one hand, Spark released funky country blues with Garland in a Chess Records mode. On the other, we also recorded Ernie Andrews, the great jazz vocalist, with a moaning Hammond B3 organ.

Probably the most meaningful things that came out of Spark, though, centered on the Robins, an early LA-based R&B group who had been around since the forties.

Leiber Our first record ever released had been the Robins singing "That's What the Good Book Says" in 1951. A little later, we wrote "Ten Days in Jail," which they recorded for RCA. When we began Spark, the Robins were the first act we signed.

Grady Chapman, who sang lead on "Whadaya Want?" was a light-skinned brother with freckles. His voice was a natural high tenor, not a falsetto. While his singing style was sweet, his personal style was tough. When he missed a session, as he often did, it was, according to the other Robins, because of run-ins with the law.

During one of those times, Grady was replaced by Carl Gardner. When Grady returned, Carl stayed, and at times the Robins became a sextet.

Ty Terrell and the Richards brothers, Billy and Roy, all wore their hair in a conk. Bobby Nunn provided the strong bass. And Carl, the newcomer from Tyler, Texas, had an exquisite tenor voice and hoped to become a great ballad singer.

The Robins were a perfect vehicle for Leiber and Stoller musical productions. Five voices to consider. Five voices to harmonize. Five voices, five characters, five actors, a veritable repertory company.

Actors deserve a great play. My main dramatic touchstones were the radio plays I heard as a kid, especially *Gang Busters*. *Gang Busters* had a dynamite opening—a siren followed by a burst of gunfire, and the announcer hyping this week's episode. I was in love with *Gang Busters* as a ten-year-old back in Baltimore, but now I was twenty. I couldn't remember any of the stories, but those sounds were still in my mind.

On July the second nineteen fifty-three
I was servin' time for armed robbery
At four o'clock in the morning I was sleepin' in my cell
I heard a whistle blow then I heard somebody yell
There's a riot goin' on . . .
Up in cell block #9

The trouble started in cell block #4
Spread like fire across the prison floor
I said, "Okay, boys, get ready to run
Here come the warden with a tommy gun."

The chorus was sung by all the Robins, but the verses were spoken. This was a monologue that had to be dramatized with great gravitas.

Stoller   We can't and won't claim credit as the inventors of rap, but if you listen to our early output, you'll hear lots of black men talking poem-stories over a heavy backbeat. When Jerry performed the songs, he gave the singers the taste and texture we were after. Bobby Nunn tried to imitate Jerry but lacked a certain flair. So we called in Richard Berry, who was one of the Flairs. Richard, who will always be remembered as the author of "Louie Louie," had the insinuating deep voice we were looking for and the attitude to go with it. He was mocking, mischievous, and funny as hell.

Looking back, it's clear that "Riot in Cell Block #9" was a radically different form of song. It would be the template for many of our biggest hits, first with the Robins and then with the Coasters. But at the moment of creation, we were too busy laughing to realize what was happening. We were merely putting a different spin on what was, after all, nothing more than the blues. Bessie Smith had her "Empty Bed Blues," Pee Wee Crayton had his "Blues After Hours," and now the Robins had the blues in a prison cell block.

The cell block was a breakout.

Leiber The Robins got it. The Robins started rocking out on almost everything we gave them: "Loop de Loop Mambo," a spoof on the raging mambo craze; "Whadaya Want?"; "The Hatchet Man" ("I been swinging so long they call me the hatchet man . . . now if you got sixty minutes, call up Lovin' Dan, but if you want some chopping call the hatchet man"). Another rap took the form of a police drama. We called it "Framed" and gave it a subtext that, despite the humor, refers to the legal brutality that impacted the black community.

Our last release on Spark lasted longest. On the corner of Beverly Boulevard and La Cienega, right in the middle of LA, was a pumping oil well. Next to the well was a beanery, Smokey Joe's. I was intrigued by the juxtaposition of the oil well and the greasy spoon.

> *One day while I was eatin' beans at Smokey Joe's Café*
> *just sittin' diggin' all the scenes at Smokey Joe's Café*
> *a chick came walkin' through the door*
> *that I had never seen before*
> *at least I never saw her down at Smokey Joe's Café*
> *and I started shakin' when she sat right down next to me*

Carl Gardner sang a perfect lead.

If you had asked me and Mike back then, we would have said that we loved the recording, that it might even be a hit, but we assumed

that in a few months the song—and, for that matter, all our songs—
would be, like a pile of old comic books, discarded and forgotten.

Stoller At the time of "Smokey Joe's Café," we had moved
our office from Crenshaw to Melrose Avenue, just west of La Cienega. It was another small storefront. That's where we rehearsed
"Smokey Joe's." We were next door to Al Berkman, a vocal coach

*From left, Jerry, Lester Sill, Lou Krefetz (manager of the Clovers)
and Mike, outside the Quintet Music office, Melrose Avenue,
Los Angeles, 1956.*

who would come out complaining that we were making too much noise. "I'm trying to train a future opera star!" he screamed.

Leiber I screamed back at the coach, "Hey, bring her in here. We'll teach her how to sing."

Stoller "Smokey Joe's Café" was important. Jerry and I were finding our voice in musical forms that, while still blues-based, had a humorous pop edge. They were still rhythm & blues written for black singers, but we were loosening up and having fun.

Life in the studio was great, but the business side wasn't. Some of our songs made a dent on the R&B charts, but only in California. We lacked national distribution. Our publishing company was seeing very little income. Lester Sill was used to this, but my father was not, and he grew increasingly nervous watching our cash flow dwindle down to practically nothing. My father wanted out.

Jerry and I weren't sure what to do. Lester was also at a loss. We needed help and direction. It came, improbably enough, from the eldest son of a Turkish diplomat who had inserted himself in the center of the LA jazz scene—Nesuhi Ertegun.

Leiber I'm sure you've heard the Ertegun story before, but it's usually told with Ahmet as the central hero. My hero was his brother Nesuhi. We met him shortly after we started Spark, while Mike and I were still running the South Central streets, going from club to club, soaking up the music and having a ball. I bumped into Nesuhi one night in 1954 at the home of Jimmy Tolbert, a nephew of Lester Young and a law student at USC, who later headed up the NAACP in Southern California. All the jazz cats hung at Jimmy's, not to mention the most beautiful black chicks. At the time, both Mike and I had black girlfriends, and I believe Jimmy's pad is where we met them.

Nesuhi was there shooting pool. He was a dapper man of great confidence and singular style. He spoke a half dozen languages, but was most conversant in the black slang that I found so alluring. He had studied at the Sorbonne; he had read Sartre and Nietzsche; he could discuss the emerging school of the abstract expressionist artists; but mostly he knew jazz. And blues. He knew some of the songs Mike and I had written and produced and was generous in his praise.

"Matter of fact, Leiber," he said, "I'd like to get to know you better."

"Sounds great."

"Hey, man, have you ever been on a honeymoon?"

"Is that a proposal?" I asked.

"No," he said. "I'm getting married and we're going to a resort for our honeymoon. I'm just imagining that I might be bored during the day and could use a tennis partner. I hear that you play."

"I do, but don't you want to be alone on your honeymoon?"

"Honeymoons are great," said Nesuhi, "but it's too much of a good thing."

"Doesn't your fiancée play tennis?"

"No, but she looks and swims like Esther Williams. You'll love her. How about it?"

"What have I got to lose?" I asked.

"Your pride. I'm an excellent tennis player and I hate losing."

So a couple of weeks later, the day after Nesuhi's wedding, off we went to Laguna Beach. It was quite a trio: Leiber at five foot eight; Nesuhi at five foot four; Nesuhi's wife, Betty, at six foot one.

During the days, Betty swam while Nesuhi and I batted the ball back and forth over the net. In the evenings, the couple disappeared while I haunted the hotel bar, chatting up the local talent.

Stoller   Nesuhi was great. Not only was he a brilliant music scholar and producer, he also taught jazz history at UCLA, the first such course at an American university. His tastes were catholic. He loved Jerry's singing, for example, and urged him to record. But of course, Jerry had this notion of authenticity and said, "I'll keep to writing."

"That writing," Nesuhi told us both, "is really something else. I've been listening to everything you've done on Spark. There are any number of hit songs that never became hits. And this new one, 'Smokey Joe's Café,' is nothing short of sensational. Let me be frank: You guys are superb songwriters. You know what you're doing in the studio. But you don't know how to distribute or sell. My brother Ahmet does. Why don't you let me call him and make an introduction?"

Leiber   In the mid-fifties, Ahmet Ertegun and his partners, Herb Abramson and Jerry Wexler, had already attained something of legendary status among the small R&B labels. Atlantic Records was the standard of quality. Atlantic had enjoyed huge hits with Stick McGhee's "Drinkin' Wine Spo-Dee-O-Dee," Ruth Brown's "Teardrops from My Eyes," and Joe Turner's "Chains of Love," which was written by Ahmet. Ahmet had also just signed Ray Charles, whose "I Got a Woman" was a radical mix of gospel and blues. Atlantic was at the forefront, and we wanted to be there with them.

"Please make the introduction," I told Nesuhi, who called his brother that day.

I spoke to all the Atlantic executives over the phone—Ahmet, Wexler, and Abramson. They couldn't have been any more cordial or eager to sign us. Within a short period of time, a deal was in place.

We would make records that Atlantic would release and promote. For that they'd pay us a royalty. We would co-publish the songs we wrote and, of course, Mike and I would get our writers' royalties. The new joint publishing company was called Tiger Music because Ahmet said it sounded lucky. Mike and I were so proud to be part of the great label that we put a sign on our office that said, "West Coast Division, Atlantic Records, Atco Records and Cat Records." (Atco and Cat were Atlantic's two subsidiaries.) Our deal was fair. In fact, it was even historic; we became the first writer-producers to get a freelance arrangement with a label. Spark was history. But that was okay. We were never in love with the idea of running a record label anyway. Now we were convinced we were heading into good times.

Hard Times

Stoller

> *I've got pains in my head, dead on my feet*
> *My pantry's empty, I ain't eaten for a week*
> *Hard times, oooh, I feel so bad*
> *When I lost my baby, I lost everything I had . . .*

Those are the lyrics to "Hard Times," our song recorded by Charles Brown in 1952. Three years later, just as our career seemed to be getting somewhere, the tone of this dark blues seemed to reflect my feelings.

In a way, I had been losing my mother for years. Her lifelong depression was mysterious and tenacious. I didn't understand it and neither did my dad. We were still living in the dark ages of mental illness, when neurobiological aspects of the disease remained undetected. The depression simply deepened, a situation that set my father increasingly on edge. The more he yelled at my mother, the more she withdrew. Both my parents were lost in confusion and pain. Looking back, no one is to blame. My parents were helpless in the face of a nameless ailment. The frustration was enormous and the tension in our household was a terrible burden for everyone.

Just as I wanted out of the household, Dad wanted me to stay. I served as a buffer between him and Mom, a position I hated. I wanted to escape. And then I met Meryl through Mom. Among my mother's artistic gifts was the ability to paint. In fact, Meryl had come by the house to buy one of Mom's paintings. Meryl and I found that we shared similar political views as well as a fascination with science fiction writers like Isaac Asimov and Ray Bradbury.

Meryl Cohen had endured a challenging childhood. Her father had died when she was four or five, and her mother, desperately poor, placed Meryl and her younger brother in an orphanage. Later she watched all her cousins go to college while, unable to afford the tuition, she went to work.

Somehow Meryl emerged from this difficult background as a very caring and good person. With her, I saw the possibility of forming my own family, away from my parents. We married a week after my twenty-second birthday in March of 1955 and then took off for Mexico on a honeymoon.

Leiber   Marriage was not my style—at least not in 1955.

In 1955, my style was hanging out at Sy Devore's on Vine Street, where George Burns and Sammy Davis, Jr., bought their silk suits and where a gentleman could get a haircut, a manicure, and a connection in the back room with one of Mickey Cohen's best bookmakers. My style was also to hang out with Vince Edwards, an aspiring singer and superb car mechanic, later to gain fame and fortune as Dr. Ben

Casey on TV. He's the guy who tuned up my Jag XK120—the first thing I bought with my Atlantic royalties—at his foreign car garage on Santa Monica Boulevard.

"Careful, Jerry," he said when I picked it up after a major overhaul. "I've retooled the engine. This baby can fly."

A couple of speeding tickets later, I saw what he meant. Vince had souped up the engine to where it was the talk of the sports car crowd. Sometimes that crowd congregated in Frank Sinatra's old haunt, Villa Capri.

One night I was there alone, drinking at the bar, when a young guy asked me my name.

"Jerry Leiber," I said.

"I thought so. You have a Jag, don't you?"

"I do."

"And you write songs."

"I do."

"I heard about your car. And that song called 'Hound Dog.'"

I looked at this guy with a little more scrutiny. He was wearing a cowboy hat pulled down to his eyes. But his eyes gave him away.

"You're that kid, aren't you?" I asked.

"What kid is that?"

"The Dean kid."

He nodded his head.

I'd seen him in Elia Kazan's film of Steinbeck's *East of Eden*. He played against Julie Harris and he was sensational. *Rebel Without a Cause* and *Giant* hadn't come out yet, but on the basis of *Eden* alone, everyone in Hollywood was talking about James Dean.

Now I suddenly felt like I was in a James Dean movie, especially when he asked me, "Wanna see what your Jag will do against my Porsche?"

"I'm too tired to drive to the desert."

"Forget the desert, Leiber," he said. "I like the freeway."

"I don't. Not for racing."

I accepted his offer of a Camel and another drink. In my mind, I played with the notion of racing James Dean.

"I have an idea," I said. "I live at the top of Laurel Canyon. On the way up, there's a street bordering the main road that's separated by a long narrow island. That street is one way coming down."

"That's where you wanna race?" asked Dean.

"Only we go one-way going up."

"And I presume there's hardly ever traffic coming down."

"Usually deserted," I assured him.

"'Usually,'" he repeated, "but not always."

"Nothing is always," I said.

"Well, it sounds interesting, Leiber. You in for a grand?"

I hesitated.

"That too heavy for you?"

"I can handle it," I said as if it were no problem.

We left the bar and went to the parking lot. He introduced me to the silver Porsche 550 Spyder that he called "Little Bastard." He checked over my Jag, then followed me up the backstreets of Laurel Canyon until we came to the foot of the hill. We parked, got out, and inspected the raceway. A few seconds later, a Ford station wagon came barreling down the street.

"Thought you said there wasn't any traffic," said Dean.

"*Hardly* any," I said.

As we stood there, though, over the next five minutes at least six cars came zooming down the hill.

"You're crazy, Leiber. Let's go back and drink."

I laughed and we drove back to Villa Capri.

"It was a setup," Dean said when we assumed our old positions at the bar. "You didn't want to race, so you proposed an impossible course."

"I did want to race," I said. "It just so happened that the course was in use."

Dean gave me one of his Actors Studio smiles that meant whatever you wanted it to mean.

I excused myself to go to the bathroom. When I got back, Dean was gone.

Two weeks later I heard the news on the radio: On his way out to a car rally in Salinas, Dean, along with his car mechanic, got into an accident. Dean's Porsche was wrecked. Dean's mechanic survived, but Dean didn't. He was dead at twenty-four.

Stoller

Back from Mexico, Meryl and I rented a rear house off Echo Park Avenue. Meryl got a job as bookkeeper at Pacific Jazz Records. I loved it when she came home with new releases by Gerry Mulligan, Chico Hamilton, Chet Baker, and one by singer Kitty White with Corky Hale playing harp.

Then bad news. A few months later, the call came: my mother, whose depression had become intolerable, swallowed a large quantity of barbiturates. All attempts to resuscitate her failed. She was gone.

We went to the funeral home and to the graveside: Mom's four older siblings, my sister and her husband, my dad and his siblings.

I wept with all of them and then for weeks to follow.

Leiber

My hard times had to do with an episode that, over years later, I'm still trying to process. It shook me to the core of my soul.

It began with a celebration, the marriage of a former girlfriend in Beverly Hills. The ceremony was short and the party was fun, but I left feeling a little strange. Why is she getting married and not me? Should she be marrying *me* and not *him*? If I wanted her, could I have had her? Did I, in fact, want her?

My mind was muddled and also a little high on champagne. Driving home, I stopped at a jazz club. I felt the need to reconsider my position in life, and a jazz club was the right place to do just that. My partnership with Mike and our songwriting success had given me some status. That felt good. Cool jazz always helped take off the edge. Shorty Rogers, the trumpeter, with drummer Shelly Manne, bassist Leroy Vinnegar, and pianist Lou Levy—the best of the West Coast cats were performing. They even played "Bernie's Tune," the song Mike and I had put lyrics to. Life could be better, but it wasn't bad.

I was nursing a drink, digging the music, when I noticed two black chicks noticing me. I nodded and smiled. They nodded and smiled back. Naturally, I was intrigued. One was my age—twenty-two or twenty-three—and the other older, perhaps thirty. They were dressed tastefully and provocatively. The younger woman was slim with long shapely legs. The older had a fine full figure. When I sent drinks to their table, they raised their glasses in my direction. I raised mine in kind and invited them over. They were happy to join me, especially the older one. She was a talker, while her younger friend was shy.

"You like jazz?" asked the older chick.

"Love it," I answered.

"Been here before?"

"Many times. Can't get enough of this group."

"Well," she said, "we're music fans ourselves. Jazz, blues—you name it."

"I'm glad you're here," I reiterated.

"We are too. We couldn't be happier."

The happiness expanded with another round of drinks. Our discussion expanded as well. They asked about my work, and I told them. They were impressed. I thought they would be. Hell, *I* was impressed with my work.

It didn't take long for the older woman to get to the point.

"Listen," she said, "you wanna party?"

"Indeed I do."

Out in the parking lot, they wanted to ride in my Jag and come to my place. The Jag was a two-seater. My place was a small house in Laurel Canyon. My heart was beating fast.

We piled in and headed up the hill, the older in the seat against the door, the younger in the middle, where the gearshift and my mind were between her legs. When we got to my place, I thought I was ready but I wasn't. That morning I had worked out at Harvey Easton's gym, overdid it, and got sick. I thought that was behind me, but it wasn't. Suddenly I felt a wave of sharp pain move over my neck and down my back. I could hardly move, much less boogie.

"What's wrong?" asked the woman in charge. "Chickening out?"

"I'm feeling bad," I said. "This isn't a good time to party."

"Tough," she said. "A deal's a deal. If you can't party, you still gotta pay."

"For what?"

"For me not walking out on the front lawn and yelling 'Rape!'"

"How much?" I asked.

"Two hundred."

"I only got twenty."

"Then get the other $180."

"I can't."

"Then watch me start screaming 'Rape!'"

"I got an idea," I said. "I got a friend who runs the Melody Club just down the hill. He has money. We'll drive down there and you'll get paid."

"Call and make sure your friend is there with the money."

I called Jake the Snake, Lester's pal and our investor in Spark. Jake always had cash. When I explained the situation, Jake wasn't sympathetic. "Throw the cunts off the mountain," he said.

"Please, Jake. Let's resolve this peacefully."

"Peace ain't my style, Jer, but for Lester's sake, I'm gonna help you out."

"My friend is waiting," I told the women, "so let's get in the car and I'll get you your money."

We piled back in the Jag, back in our same positions—the older one against the door, the leggy one in the middle. My back, neck, and shoulders were screaming in pain. Patches of fog blurred my vision. I proceeded slowly.

"Get moving," urged the lady in charge.

The road was tricky, curvy, and treacherous even under the best conditions.

"Get going," she said, "or I'll drive this motherfucker myself."

I sped up but then slowed down. The road was slicker than I had anticipated. In slowing down, I tried to downshift, but the girl's crotch and the gearshift were tangled up. If I hadn't been in pain, that might have been sexy or funny. Now it was neither. Instead of engaging the gearshift, I had to hit the brakes, and when I hit the brakes the car started to slide off the road, and as it slid, it spun out of control. Suddenly all hell broke loose: We crashed off an embankment where the front weight of the car carried us down, down, down—off the embankment down the mountain, sixteen, seventeen, eighteen feet straight down to where the car smashed into a tree, rolled, and flipped. I held on to the steering wheel with such strength that when the car hit the tree both my elbows hit my thighs, leaving huge black-and-blue marks. Aside from those marks, I didn't have a scratch. The woman by the door was thrown from the car but virtually uninjured.

When I looked at the young lady in the middle, though, my heart stopped: the car's modular frame had caved in and crushed her skull. She was dead.

Someone called the cops, who showed up in no time. They patted me down.

"When did you jump out?" asked the cop in charge.

"I didn't," I said, so badly shaken I could hardly talk.

"You had to. The doors are jammed closed."

"I crawled out of a shattered window," I said.

"We'll see what the judge says," said the cop, "unless you want to settle it here and now. I can write up the report any way you want it written."

The cop was playing me for a bribe. I couldn't fathom it. A woman had been killed. I had no stomach for making any deals. I refused. His response was to throw me in jail. I spent the night in a lockup with fifty thugs. I expected to be murdered in my sleep, so I didn't sleep at all.

A mountain of a black man came over and asked me for a smoke. I handed him the whole pack of Camels.

"I know who you are," he said. "You gonna be alright."

He kept guard over me all night.

The cops claimed I had jumped out of the car while it was moving and left the women to die. The charge was manslaughter.

A friend's dad, a big-time defense lawyer, came to see me. I described what happened. "Take off your pants," he said.

"What for?"

"Just do it."

When I did, he saw those two giant black-and-blue bruises on my thighs.

"Those bruises will save your ass," he said. "They prove you were clutching the steering wheel and digging your elbows into your thighs as the car went down. They refute the cop's report. They're all the proof you need."

The judge agreed. He threw out the case against me.

But that didn't bring the young woman back to life. I contacted her family and sent my respects. I asked for their forgiveness. I did everything I could to put the incident behind me. But I never could. I still can't.

Stoller *Five thousand dollars at one crack*, I thought to myself. *I'll probably never see that much money again.*

It was a royalty check from Capitol for "Bazoom (I Need Your Lovin')," a song we'd written that turned into a hit for the Cheers. And we had a new Cheers record out called "Black Denim Trousers and Motorcycle Boots," which was also moving up the charts. So Meryl and I, married for a year, decided to put our few possessions in storage, give up our rented house, and use the money to explore the Old World. We no longer had an address, but we'd sort that out when we got back. We were going on a three-month trip to Europe to see new sights, hear foreign languages, eat strange foods, sample exotic drinks, and walk down streets where people had walked centuries before.

The trip was mapped out: a twenty-five-hour flight from LA to Copenhagen on an SAS turbo prop plane that refueled in Winnipeg and Greenland. From Copenhagen it was on to Amsterdam, then Brussels, London, Dublin, and Paris, followed by a month motoring across France. We returned the car in Nice, took a train to Venice, and spent another month in Italy, winding up in Naples. It all went wonderfully well. The highlight of the trip was going to an Edith Piaf concert at L'Olympia in Paris where she introduced a song she later called her biggest-selling single record ever, "L'homme à la

Moto," the French version of "Black Denim Trousers and Motor-cycle Boots." The great Piaf was doing Leiber and Stoller!

The trip home promised to be still another highlight. The travel agent talked us into upgrading to a newer ship.

"What's it called?" I asked.

"The *Andrea Doria*," the agent answered. "It's beautiful. You'll never forget it."

"L'Homme a la Moto" sheet music.

That night of nights I was reading, of all things, *A Night to Remember*, the story of the sinking of the *Titanic*. The bestseller had come out in paperback and many other passengers were reading it as well.

I planned to get up early the next morning so I could be on deck as we sailed into New York Harbor. I wanted to see the Statue of Liberty and experience what my grandparents had experienced when they had first arrived in America.

A little after 11:00 p.m., July 25, 1956, Meryl suggested we go up to the cabin-class ballroom to say good-bye to several friends we had made during the voyage. I reluctantly agreed. I was drinking a glass of champagne and walking toward the card room to see if there was a poker game going on. Meryl was talking to a woman who was traveling alone. All was calm when, out of nowhere—

Boom!

The collision was thunderous.

Later we'd learn that we'd been struck in the side by the *Stockholm*, another huge ocean liner. The impact rocked everyone and everything. Immediately our ship started listing to starboard. That meant no one could get to half the lifeboats. The *Stockholm* went two-thirds of the way through the *Andrea Doria*, bounced off, and came back in again. It looked like someone had taken a giant letter opener and was ripping open the side of our ship. Due to the crash, none of the lifeboats could be deployed.

"Get up to the boat deck!" I told Meryl and the woman. "I'll try and get the life preservers from our cabin."

The woman's cabin was too far to reach, but I was able to get to our cabin. The door had been thrown open and the floor was covered with water and oil. I grabbed the two preservers and left everything else—our clothes, presents for friends, movie camera, thirty rolls of color film documenting our trip.

It was tricky navigating around the sinking ship. The story of the *Titanic* was racing around my head. Sirens were blasting and people were screaming. As I ran back to give the women the preservers, a family tried to grab one of them from me.

"Our father needs it!" they screamed.

"It's not for me," I said, tucking the preservers under my arm and barreling past them like a football halfback heading for the goal line.

I ran up to the boat deck and found Meryl and her friend. I gave them each a preserver. I figured, what the hell, I could swim. As the ship listed, we clung to the railing. We could feel it going down. After an hour, a woman from the crew came around and gave me a preserver of my own. Other than that, the crew was nowhere to be found.

Hours passed. The ship continued to sink, slowly but steadily. *This is it,* I said to myself. I considered praying. But being an atheist, that seemed to be a waste of time. Then, when we learned that other passengers were getting into lifeboats, we formed a human chain and slid down to the low side of the deck. From there Meryl and I climbed down a wildly swinging Jacob's ladder into a lifeboat.

We were seated among sixty or seventy other passengers. But a broken rudder meant that the lifeboat couldn't be steered. The boat had to be operated manually, so I began rowing with the other men.

We almost collided with a freighter that was standing by. The freighter, the *Cape Ann*, proved to be our salvation. Its crew fished us out of the lifeboat and covered us with blankets.

We were saved, but forty-six people on the *Andrea Doria* and five on the *Stockholm* were not. Years later another fourteen people would die diving to salvage what was left of the sunken ship.

After a hot breakfast of scrambled eggs and bacon prepared by the *Cape Ann* crew, I sent a telegram to Lester Sill, care of Atlantic

Records in New York. I told him to tell my father, my sister, and Jerry that I was all right.

Twelve hours after the *Cape Ann* left the scene of the collision, it pulled into New York Harbor. Small boats full of photographers and reporters were escorting us, taking photos and yelling questions to us until we docked. As I stepped off the gangplank, Jerry ran up to me, saying, "Mike, you're okay!" before adding, "We have a smash hit."

"You're kidding?"

"'Hound Dog.'"

"Big Mama Thornton?"

"No, some white kid named Elvis Presley."

9

New Times

Stoller Everything changed. My arrival in New York became a moment of departure in brand-new waters. I had found salvation in a lifeboat, and suddenly I went from sinking to rising.

After we checked into the Algonquin Hotel and rested, Meryl and I, together with Jerry, took a taxi to the Russian Tea Room on Fifty-seventh Street, where we met the Atlantic team—Ahmet and Nesuhi Ertegun, Jerry Wexler, Herb and Miriam Abramson, and Pete Kameron, who managed the Modern Jazz Quartet and other jazz artists. These were charismatic characters in the extreme—brilliant, both impressive scholars and impassioned fans of the music and, like us, early producers of a genre they loved. It was all about jazz and rhythm & blues. And like any smart label owners, it was all about hits. That's why we were greeted as conquering heroes. The Robins's "Smokey Joe's Café," the final single before Spark folded, was released by Atlantic and became our first single on their Atco subsidiary. It sold a ton of records.

Ahmet was cool and debonair. He had turned his slight Turkish

From left, Jerry Wexler, Nesuhi Ertegun, Ahmet Ertegun.

accent into a kind of self-styled hipster lingo. In an extra-dry-martini way, he was also extremely funny. In contrast, Wexler was street— New York street—and he knew a lot about black music. Wexler ran the day-to-day operation with great intensity. When we met Abramson, who had founded the label with Ahmet, Herb was on his way out. When Abramson was drafted by the military as a dentist, Wexler virtually replaced him. Herb was perhaps the most knowledgeable of the three about the blues, but he had neither the suave personality of Ahmet nor the aggressiveness of Wexler.

Meanwhile, as a character, my partner Leiber could hold his

ground—and then some—with the Atlantic bigwigs. For every quip from Ahmet or Wexler, Jerry came back with three or four of his own. The boys had met their match. I think I was seen more as the reserved piano player. I was far less vocal than Jerry.

Nesuhi and Ahmet invited Meryl and me to Basin Street to hear the Modern Jazz Quartet, whose records Nesuhi produced. They were playing songs from their recently released album. I especially loved "Django," a synthesis of elegant classical music and jazzy blues. It was a thrilling evening to cap off a perilous rescue at sea.

Leiber
I was excited to be in New York. By this point we had met many of the label owners and had no doubt that Ahmet and Jerry sat at the top of the heap. They understood exactly what they did and promised to leave us alone to do our thing. We'd write the songs and make the records; they'd sell 'em. From the start, and for several years afterward, it worked well.

As for the amazing fact that Elvis had recorded "Hound Dog," well, I had different feelings. The first feeling is the one that washes over any songwriter when he learns he has a hit: He hears the cash register ring and the Sale! sign come up. That's a good feeling. But when I heard Elvis's version, I had a bad feeling. I didn't like the way he did it. Somebody changed the lyrics. I had written:

> *You ain't nothing but a hound dog*
> *Quit snooping 'round my door*
> *You can wag your tail,*
> *But I ain't gonna feed you no more*

But Elvis sang:

You ain't nothing but a hound dog
Crying all the time
You ain't never caught a rabbit
And you ain't no friend of mine

To this day I have no idea what that rabbit business is all about. The song is not about a dog; it's about a man, a freeloading gigolo. Elvis's version makes no sense to me, and, even more irritatingly, it is not the song that Mike and I wrote. Of course, the fact that it sold more than seven million copies took the sting out of what seemed to be a capricious change of lyrics. But, lick for lick, there's no comparison between the Presley version and the Big Mama original. Elvis played with the song; Big Mama nailed it.

Elvis knew Big Mama's version, but that wasn't the one that got him to do it. He had heard it sung by a lounge act at the Sands Hotel in Vegas—Freddie Bell and the Bellboys. Apparently he liked the rhumba feel to the rhythm and told his boys to work up an arrangement. So Elvis was really covering a cover.

By virtue of that Presley cover, we were thrown into the biggest commercial revolution in American music: teenage rock and roll. In the postwar prosperity of the fifties, teenagers had money and they were restless. White teenagers had been listening to some of the rhythm & blues that Mike and I had written and produced. Elvis was the prime example. When the music was sung by one of their own, white teenagers liked it even more. That's understandable. And that's why, in gross terms, rock and roll became a mega-industry while R&B would lag behind. In its influence, R&B was always ahead. Chuck Berry, Bo Diddley, and Little Richard, not to mention Ray Charles, created the musical templates that, a half century later, are still firmly in place.

All this is to say that Mike and I got awfully goddamn lucky. We were two guys looking to write songs for black artists with black feelings rendered in black vernacular. Suddenly, the leader of the revolution known as rock and roll started covering those songs. And whether I liked his interpretation or not is beside the point. We were in the right place at the right time.

Stoller   My problem with "Hound Dog" was that I couldn't get Big Mama's version out of my mind. And I agree with Jerry that the lyric change was annoying. Watching Elvis's early performances on the *Ed Sullivan* and *Steve Allen* shows, though, I saw a guy with undeniable charisma and a kind of rhythmic irresistibility, not to mention a damn good voice. He'd be the first to tell you that, as a teenager in Memphis, he went to Beale Street and studied the great bluesmen. To have a white kid taking black blues to the top of the charts was unprecedented. Naturally, a horde of others would follow in his footsteps. But there's a world of difference between, say, Pat Boone covering Little Richard's "Tutti Frutti" and Elvis covering Big Mama or Big Bill Broonzy. Elvis had that edge of danger and mystery. Pat Boone was insipid.

Leiber   When Elvis's manager Colonel Tom Parker took his boy from Memphis independent Sun Records to the open market in 1954, Ahmet thought the $25,000 signing tag too high, so he passed. RCA scooped him up. It just so happened that our connection with Elvis coincided with our connection with Atlantic. Two major explosions in one year. Ahmet and Wexler were impressed with the sales of "Hound Dog," but they were even more impressed with those first Coasters singles we submitted to them.

Stoller

The Coasters were a spinoff from the Robins, and the Coasters were managed by Lester Sill. The name came from their West Coast origin. To Carl Gardner and Bobby Nunn of the Robins, we added Billy Guy and Leon Hughes.

Billy Guy was the comic. He had great timing and loved to play the country yokel. In real life, he was city-sharp and super-hip. Carl Gardner, as I've mentioned, was another cool cat, a great lead singer. His true ambition was to sing classy ballads. Like so many of his fellow R&B singers, Carl's goal was to become another Nat Cole or Billy Eckstine. His biggest phobias were ghosts and earthquakes. (Decades later, Carl was convinced to come to Los Angeles for a reunion concert. "Not with those earthquakes out there," he said. "Come on, Carl," he was told. "Do you know what the odds of there being an earthquake are?" The night he arrived, a major quake threw him out of his hotel bed.)

If anything, the Coasters showed even more dramatic flair than the Robins. That's largely because as directors—which is a more accurate term for what we did in the studio than "producers"—Jerry and I were more experienced. By 1956, we'd been at it five straight years. And having experimented with this new playlet form for a while, we were even more relaxed about trying new things.

"Down in Mexico," for example, the first hit under the new Coasters name, is set south of the border. It has a slight Latin tinge that's reminiscent of the Chicano milieu I had encountered in high school in LA. But the blues is all over it. And then there's Jerry's fascination with funky bars and the sexy stories they suggest:

> *Down in Mexicali*
> *There's a crazy little place that I know*
> *Where the drinks are hotter than the chili sauce*

And the boss is a cat named Joe
He wears a red bandana, plays a blues "piana"
In a honky-tonk
Down in Mexico
He wears a purple sash
And a black moustache
In a honky-tonk
Down in Mexico

Leiber   While "Hound Dog" was topping the charts, "Down in Mexico" was also making noise. Mike and I decided to stay in New York City and get better acquainted with Atlantic. Mike and Meryl and I got an apartment together on Seventy-first Street between Fifth and Madison. Mike and I wrote a few things—like "Fools Fall in Love" for the Drifters, Atlantic's biggest-selling group, and "Lucky Lips" for Ruth Brown, whose early R&B hits such as "(Mama) He Treats Your Daughter Mean" had built the label. In 1957, "Lucky Lips" was the vehicle with which Ruth crossed over to the pop charts.

But while the married couple was settling down, I was growing restless. I had a lady friend back in Los Angeles who was calling to me.

"Be back in a week or so," I told Mike.

Stoller   That week turned into months. I kept busy in New York. One day, Jerry Wexler called me to the studio to play piano for Big Joe Turner. Joe was the great Kansas City blues shouter who had broken into R&B with "Shake, Rattle and Roll." I played on Joe's 1957 "Teenage Letter." Ray Charles, who was also in the studio that day, played piano on the other side. Go figure!

Leiber "Fools Fall in Love" turned out to be a big hit for the Drifters, an R&B vocal group that would later move our professional lives in a different direction. For the present, though, those lyrics might have revealed an autobiographical subtext.

> *Fools fall in love in a hurry*
> *Fools give their hearts much too soon*
> *Just play them two bars of "Stardust"*
> *Just hang out one silly moon*

So there I was back in LA, searching for love. But love came and went. I looked for it or it looked for me, I'm not sure which. But in any event, I kept missing it.

I was intrigued by a woman named Janice. Her father was an anesthesiologist. She lived in a lovely house on Sunset Plaza Drive. She was several years younger than I was, very beautiful, yet oddly enough, I wasn't attracted to her sexually. I was more taken with the fact that she was taken with me. I suppose she thought there was this edge of danger about me—the mystery and the music of rhythm & blues. I had had affairs with other women, but Janice held a special and powerful place in my psyche. When I was in New York, she kept calling. I responded by one day showing up in LA.

That's when she told me that another man, a former high school football star, had won her heart. She had decided to marry him. *Fools fall in love in a hurry,* I thought to myself. *Fools give their hearts much too soon*. I had been a bit of a star in high school, a wrestler and gymnast. But I hadn't played football. I hadn't counted on getting to LA and having Janice reject me out of turn.

"Can I read you the lyrics of a song I've written?" I asked her.

"Of course," she said.

I quoted myself:

> *Fools fall in love just like schoolgirls*
> *Blinded by rose-colored dreams*
> *They build their castles on wishes*
> *With only rainbows for beams*

Who doesn't want to write a song about fools falling in love? Besides, isn't that a way to chase the blues away? I remember a blues singer once telling me that the best way to lose the blues is to sing them. "When you're singing, you're happy," he said. "Even if the song is sad."

I had some deep sadness inside me. I had a pretty complicated set of crossed wires and faulty connections. I had the need to talk about it and take a look at it from lots of different angles.

On the bright side, Mike was coming back to LA. It'd been several months since we'd written anything. That was way too long. Atlantic was yelling for songs. After the success of "Hound Dog," even Elvis's people were yelling for songs. It was time to get going.

"Got any ideas?" Mike asked when he arrived in California.

"A couple," I said. "A coupla thousand."

10

Searchin'

Stoller By early 1957, I had returned to LA. That's when Jerry and I went back to working with the Coasters. In those winter months we wrote two of the most successful songs of our career. In a world where white voices like Paul Anka's singing "Diana" or Debbie Reynolds's singing "Tammy" were selling records, we proved that authentic black voices like the Coasters' could sell to blacks *and* whites.

Leiber Had you told me in the winter months of 1957 that "Searchin'," for instance, had autobiographical implications, I probably would have laughed. But given the debacle with Janice, given that I was looking for romance, maybe "Searchin'" did carry a tinge of self-reflection. It was certainly reflective of those radio shows I loved as a kid. The song is thick with pop culture references:

> *Sherlock Holmes, Sam Spade, got nothin', child, on me*
> *Sergeant Friday, Charlie Chan and Boston Blackie*

No matter where she's hidin', she's gonna hear me comin'
I'm gonna walk right down that street like Bulldog Drummon'

Stoller

Besides being the Coasters' biggest hit, "Searchin'" represents the beginning of a more universal rock and roll style. We weren't aiming for a bigger audience. Rather, our aim remained the same: write the right song for the right artists. It just so happened, though, that the planet was tilting in our direction. These tales, mostly set in the ghetto and told by black characters, were suddenly appealing to everyone. "Young Blood," the ostensible A-side, hit the charts first, but it was overtaken by "Searchin'." We wound up with a two-sided hit that stayed on the charts for seven months.

Leiber

We recorded "Young Blood" in LA but wrote it in New York. Jerry Wexler had invited me to dinner to meet the family at his house in Great Neck. On the way out, he challenged me.

"Doc Pomus has a terrific title," he said.

"What is it?" I asked.

"'Young Blood.'"

"I like it."

"Can you write lyrics for it?"

"When?"

"Whenever you're in the mood."

"How far are we from your house?" I asked.

"Fifteen minutes."

"I'll have the lyrics finished before we get there."

And I did:

I saw her standing on the corner
A yellow ribbon in her hair
I couldn't keep myself from shoutin'
Look-a-there . . . look-a-there, look-a-there, look-a-there

Stoller We were listening to some playbacks at the Atlantic studios on Fifty-sixth Street when Jerry started reciting these lyrics to "Young Blood."

I went to the piano and came up with a tune. It probably took me about as long to write the music as it took Jerry to write the lyrics. I was especially pleased because I was crazy about Doc Pomus. He was the great R&B guru. Doc was actually a Jewish guy whose real name was Jerome Felder. He'd had polio as a child and walked with the aid of braces. When I met him in 1956, I immediately sang him the jingle that I remembered him doing on the commercial for Alley's Pants Shop, a haberdashery in Brooklyn. I'd heard it on Symphony Sid's radio show when I was a kid in Queens and still remembered the lyrics.

Alley, Alley, Alley
You're so good to me
You got those three-ring bottoms . . .

A year earlier, at the same time that Joe Turner recorded Doc's "Boogie Woogie Country Girl," Joe had also sung "The Chicken and the Hawk," a high-flying blues Jerry and I had written about the perils of love:

A curly-headed chicken fell in love with a chicken hawk
Fell head over heels for that hawk's sweet talk

She said, "Take me up, hawky, take me up in the sky
I'm just a little bitty chicken and I don't know how to fly"

Leiber The Coasters' artistic and commercial brilliance
was becoming increasingly evident to Wexler and Ertegun. They
kept urging us to get back to New York so we could work with their
entire stable of artists. But the thing that really got us back was Elvis.
Jean (pronounced "Gene") Aberbach, Elvis's music publisher, had

Jerry with bassist Joe Comfort, Radio Recorders
studio, Hollywood, 1957.

been on our case to write more songs for the man we still hadn't met. Jean and his brother Julian were Viennese immigrants who spoke with heavy accents and had built Hill and Range Songs into an international publishing empire, primarily based on country and western songs. Jean's relationship with Elvis's manager, Colonel Tom Parker, had begun with country singer Eddy Arnold.

After "Hound Dog" hit big, Aberbach wanted another Leiber-Stoller smash for Elvis. I came up with a wild idea that was half-joke and half-serious. I thought of a song we'd put out on Spark, "Love Me," by Willy and Ruth. It had been covered by everyone from Georgia Gibbs to Billy Eckstine. Actually we'd written it as a parody of a corny hillbilly ballad:

> *Treat me like a fool*
> *Treat me mean and cruel*
> *But love me*

> *Break my faithful heart*
> *Tear it all apart*
> *But love me*

Corny or not, we sent it over to Elvis's people. Lo and behold, Aberbach liked it, and so did Freddy Bienstock, Aberbach's cousin and the professional manager of Elvis's music company. Elvis recorded it and "Love Me" turned into one of the big records of 1956.

Stoller   Of course, '56 was the big breakthrough for Elvis. He left Sun and joined RCA where, in the first year, he had "Heartbreak Hotel," "Blue Suede Shoes," "I Want You, I Need You, I Love

You," "Don't Be Cruel," and "Love Me Tender"—plus our "Hound Dog" and "Love Me."

Although we hadn't been crazy about his interpretation of "Hound Dog," we were tremendously impressed with his performance of "Love Me." Then there was "Loving You," a ballad we wrote that became the title song of his next film. In 1957 we got another call from Jean Aberbach after we had gone back to work on new material for the Coasters in LA.

"Come to New York," said Aberbach. "We want you to write songs for Elvis's new film."

So back we flew to the Big Apple.

Leiber We probably should have taken the assignment a little more seriously. There we were, two twenty-three-year-old guys, in a suite at the Gorham Hotel in the middle of Manhattan, itching for action. We ran to see Miles Davis at the Village Vanguard. Basie was at Birdland, Monk was at the Five Spot. Then of course there were drinks—lots of drinks—and dinners with Wexler, Ahmet, and Nesuhi.

Stoller We were having a ball, seeing Broadway shows, visiting museums, and enjoying everything the city had to offer. Aberbach gave us the script for the new movie, but for a week it lay unopened along with the tourist magazines provided by the hotel. We had had an upright piano delivered to our suite—just in case inspiration hit. So far, though, it hadn't.

Leiber Jason Robards was doing a revival of O'Neill's *Long Day's Journey into Night*. It was the era of Arthur Miller's and Tennessee Williams's great plays. Who could stay cooped up in a hotel with so much happening out on the streets?

Stoller Aberbach wanted results, so he came by the hotel one day at 1:00 p.m. We were sitting in the living room, devouring a big breakfast.

"Well, boys, where are my songs?" he asked.

"Don't worry, Jean," we said. "You'll get them."

"Oh, I'm not worrying," he said, "because I'm not leaving until I have them." And with that, he pushed the large sofa from the center of the room against the door, thus preventing any exit. Then he sat on the sofa and dozed off.

Jerry and I lit up cigarettes—cigarette smoking was a mandatory part of our writing process—found the script and leafed through it. I sat at the piano and started playing. Jerry sat in an easy chair and started throwing out ideas. By 6:00 p.m., we'd written four songs: "Jailhouse Rock," "Treat Me Nice," "(You're So Square) Baby I Don't Care," and "I Want to Be Free," which had a double meaning for us at the time.

Just about then, Aberbach stretched and rubbed his eyes.

"Okay, Jean," said Jerry, "here they are."

"Good," Aberbach said as he got up, moved the couch from the door, and set us free.

A month or so later we were back in LA, face to face with the world's most famous rock and roller. The King had requested our presence.

In the King's Court

Stoller   I guess it must have been in April of '57 that we met Colonel Parker for the first time. It happened over dinner at the Beverly Hills Hotel. Jean Aberbach was the conduit.

"The Colonel wants to see you in person before you meet Elvis," said Jean.

"Is this an audition?" I asked.

"The Colonel is very careful about who he lets into Elvis's circle."

"I'm very careful about who I have dinner with," said Jerry.

Jean didn't laugh. "Just be on your best behavior," he told us both.

Leiber   Of course, the Colonel wasn't really a colonel. He was Thomas A. Parker, whose former job as a carnival barker defined his personality. He had a definite shtick ("Pick a number from one to

"Jailhouse Rock" *sheet music.*

ten"). He told dozens of canned jokes. I can't remember any of them except that they weren't funny. But it didn't matter that we didn't laugh, because the Colonel wasn't really conscious of us. Of course, he knew we were the songwriters of "Hound Dog" and the new songs for *Jailhouse Rock*. He knew more hit songs for Elvis meant more money for him. Beyond that, though, he was more interested in putting on his own show than getting to know us.

He had his long cigar and his confected Southern accent. He was fat and smart and a nonstop talker whose ego was always on parade. He told us in great detail all he had done for Elvis—and all he intended to do.

"Elvis," he said, "is going to be bigger than the president, bigger than the pope."

Naturally we agreed.

Stoller The Colonel had the kind of energy that sucked all the air out of the room, even the dining room at the Beverly Hills Hotel. I had little interest in the man. Elvis was the guy we were eager to meet. The session was due to start later that week.

Leiber My heterosexual credits have long been established, so I can comfortably say that the first thing that hit me when I walked into the recording studio and found myself standing next to Elvis Presley was his physical beauty. Far more than his pictures, his actual presence was riveting. He had a shy smile and quiet manner that were disarming.

All this happened at Radio Recorders Annex, the same studio

where Big Mama had recorded "Hound Dog" back in August of 1952. Elvis wanted us there to produce the songs for the soundtrack we'd written for him.

Stoller

It's important to remember that on the day we met Elvis, he was twenty-two and we were twenty-four. We were contemporaries. Remember, too, that Jerry and I shared the uppity view that he and I were among the few white guys who knew about the blues. In the first five minutes of conversation with Elvis, we learned we were dead wrong.

Elvis knew the blues. He was a Ray Charles fanatic and even knew that Ray had sung our song "The Snow Is Falling." In fact, he knew virtually all of our songs. There wasn't any R&B he didn't know. He could quote from Arthur "Big Boy" Crudup, B.B. King, and Big Bill Broonzy.

Leiber

When it came to the blues, Elvis knew his stuff. He may not have been conversant about politics or world history, but his blues knowledge was almost encyclopedic. Mike and I were blown away. In fact, the conversation got so enthusiastic that Mike and Elvis sat down at the piano and started playing four-handed blues. He definitely felt our passion for the real roots material and shared that passion with all his heart. Just like that, we fell in love with the guy.

"Let's get started," Elvis said. "Let's cut some records."

We jumped right into "Jailhouse Rock." The initial idea was just to show up at the studio to meet Elvis. But, as naturally as the winter turns to spring, we found ourselves in charge of the session. We were producing the guy. Mike worked out the arrangement with Elvis's band—Bill Black on upright bass, Scotty Moore on guitar, D.J. Fontana on drums, and Dudley Brooks on piano. As far as the vocals went, I was amazed to see that Elvis was happy to hear me sing the song with what I considered the right attitude. He was following my vocal cues.

Stoller Elvis was completely open and never acted like a diva. When it was time to do the actual recording, Jerry was in the control

From left, Mike, Elvis and Jerry. Culver City, California, 1957.

booth and I stayed on the floor. I played piano on one cut, and Jerry, with his unique style of body language, conducted Elvis's vocals.

The other thing that amazed us was that no one was rushing us to get through. During a recording session, Jerry and I were used to watching the clock. The musicians' union allowed four songs in three hours or you got into the dreaded overtime. On Elvis's sessions, though, those restrictions were lifted. The Jordanaires (Elvis's backup vocal quartet), the guys in the band and Elvis's paid companions (the so-called Memphis Mafia) would order lunch— peanut butter sandwiches and orange pop—while the clock kept ticking.

Sometimes we'd do two or three takes on a song; sometimes up to twenty-five. And yet, even in this relaxed atmosphere, by evening time we'd cut three songs.

At the end of the day, Elvis was as high on the music as Jerry and I. That was a Wednesday. Elvis didn't show up at the studio on Thursday, but he was back on Friday to do the fourth song, "(You're So Square) Baby I Don't Care."

Leiber The fourth song was the most fun because by then Elvis was deep into our producing style. Our style wasn't anything more than being loose and having fun.

Elvis's initial shyness had totally melted away and he was completely in the spirit of the music. He actually picked up an electric bass and kicked off the intro to "Baby I Don't Care." It also pleased me no end that even when I thought we had a perfect vocal take, Elvis would want to do another—and then another. Each one would be better. He was digging deep and coming up with great new ammunition.

On our final day at Radio Recorders, when we had all gotten friendly and were listening to the playbacks, Elvis was slapping us on the back and telling us we were the baddest cats in town. A couple of the guys from MGM dropped by and listened as well. Elvis was singing our praises when one of the men—he might have been the casting director—looked at me and said, "He looks like a piano player."

"He's not," said Elvis. "That's Leiber. Leiber writes the lyrics."

"Well, he still looks like a piano player," the casting director repeated.

"The piano player's over there," said Elvis, pointing to Mike. "He writes the music."

"How 'bout if we get Leiber to play the part of the piano player in the movie?" asked the casting director. "All he has to do is run his fingers over the keys. Any fool can do that."

"Thank you," I said, "for the vote of confidence. But Mike's the piano player."

"No, you go ahead, Jerry," said Mike in his customarily generous manner. "This is your big break. I don't want to deny you your screen debut."

So it was set: *Jailhouse Rock,* starring Elvis Presley and introducing Jerry Leiber.

Stoller

On the morning that filming was to begin, Jerry called me.

"I got a problem. I can't make it," he said.

"Why?" I asked.

"I'm dying."

"Well, dying is definitely a problem. What's wrong, Jer?"

"A toothache from hell. You gotta replace me."

"But they want *you*," I reminded him.

"They'll never know the difference."

When I got to MGM Studios, they told me to shave off my goatee.

"It's a scene stealer," they said.

I showed up on the soundstage, went to wardrobe, where they put me in a Hawaiian shirt. I ended up in all the scenes where Elvis sang with the band. I never uttered a word. I wasn't allowed to. Because I wasn't in the Screen Actors Guild, I couldn't talk on screen.

Naturally, Elvis was the focus of attention. You couldn't help but notice his naturalness and ease as an actor. Yet, on at least one occasion, I noticed something else: his underlying insecurity.

Mike, playing piano for Elvis in Jailhouse Rock, *1957.*

It happened when Elvis walked through an area where the extras and bit-part players were sitting around. As he passed by, someone told a joke and everyone began to laugh. Elvis wheeled around and angrily said, "I bet you think you're really hot."

He had thought they were laughing at him. They weren't. I know; I was there. Elvis walked away, mumbling.

One day he approached me as we were leaving the set.

"Mike," he said, "I want you to write me a real pretty ballad."

"I'll get right on it."

That was on a Friday.

Saturday morning, Jerry and I got together and wrote "Don't." On Sunday, we got Young Jessie of the Flairs to sing the demo in an

Mike at Radio Recorders studio with
Young Jesse, Hollywood, 1957.

Elvis-like mode. (Jessie had recently substituted for Leon Hughes on the Coasters' recordings of "Searchin'" and "Young Blood.")

I brought "Don't" to Elvis on the set that Monday. He liked it, recorded it, and by January of the following year—1958—it hit #1, only three months after "Jailhouse Rock" had also gone to the top. You'd think we'd be heroes. But in the court of the King, it didn't work that way.

Leiber   I get a call from Freddy Bienstock.

"What is your partner doing giving a song to Elvis Presley?" he asks. Freddy sounds enraged.

"Has Elvis decided to stop singing?" I ask.

"No, that's not the point." Now Freddy's yelling.

"Freddy," I say, "what's the problem, man? Did Elvis hate the song?"

"No, the problem is that he likes it."

"That's a problem?" I ask.

"It is when we don't have a contract. Nothing's written down. You just don't hand a song to Elvis without a contract. In fact, you don't hand a song to Elvis at all. You hand a song to me or to Jean Aberbach. Then we get the business straight first."

"Well, when Mike and I wrote the song, we presumed the business would be the same as all business with Elvis. The Colonel is going to demand that Elvis and the Aberbachs own the publishing rights, right?"

"Right."

"And we'll give them the publishing rights, just like before. So again I ask the question: what's the problem?"

"It's a question of procedure. The Colonel hates it when anyone goes behind his back."

"Mike didn't go behind his back. Mike's a straight shooter. Mike's the original straight shooter. Elvis asked him to write a ballad for him and we did. Beginning and end of story."

"You still don't get it."

"Maybe I don't want to get it, Freddy. But it really doesn't matter because Elvis has the ballad he asked for. And he'll have another hit. And all's well that ends well."

"If only it were that easy."

"It is, man," I say. "Believe me, it is."

Stoller   Another critical Colonel moment came during the shooting of *Jailhouse Rock*.

After a long day on the soundstage, Elvis invited me back to the Beverly Wilshire, where he was staying. He'd had a pool table set up in his suite.

"Wanna shoot a game?" Elvis asked me.

"Sure," I said.

This was after he'd recorded our four songs for the soundtrack and after I'd given him "Don't." At this point Elvis was a big Leiber and Stoller fan and was telling everyone we were his "good luck charms."

"Whenever I record," he said, "I want you guys in the studio. You're the guys who make the magic."

Music to my ears.

Elvis's companions, the Memphis Mafia, were all there. They were drinking Cokes and waiting for their turn at the pool table. On the radio, the DJ was playing "Ruby Baby," a song we'd written for the Drifters. Elvis was actually singing along with the record:

> *I've got a gal and Ruby is her name*
> *Ruby Ruby Ruby Baby*
> *She don't love me, but I love her just the same*
> *Ruby Ruby Ruby Baby*
> *Ruby Ruby how I want ya*
> *Like a ghost I'm gonna haunt ya*
> *Ruby Ruby, when will you be mine*

"Hey, Mike," said Elvis, "how do you guys write all these great songs?"

"Well, Elvis," I said, "we just kinda sit down and jam."

"It's amazing to me. I guess I just ain't much of a writer."

"You don't have to write songs. You're Elvis."

With that, Elvis gave me one of those gosh-darn expressions. At that point in his career, he was still humble.

As our game went on, I was taking careful aim at the nine ball, trying to sink it and not scratch. I looked up for a second and suddenly there was no one in the room but me. Where the hell had everyone gone?

A couple of minutes went by. When Elvis returned, his head was down and his demeanor totally changed.

"I'm really sorry, Mike," he said, "but you're gonna have to leave. The Colonel came in and he doesn't want anyone here but me and the guys."

"Okay," I said, not wanting to make any more trouble. And with that, I left.

The next day at the shoot I mentioned the incident to one of Elvis's Memphis buddies.

"Don't take it personally, Mike," he said. "It's just that the Colonel doesn't want Elvis to develop a friendship with anyone but us."

Leiber A couple of months after *Jailhouse Rock* wrapped, Mike and I were still living in LA when we got a frantic call from Freddy Bienstock.

"Elvis is cutting a Christmas album," he said, "and they're a song short. He wants you guys to write something for him."

"When?"

"Today."

Next thing I know, Mike and I are driving over to Radio Recorders on Santa Monica Boulevard. When we walk in, Elvis is all smiles.

"My good luck charms are back!" He's beaming.

The Colonel is scowling.

"You got the song?" the Colonel wants to know.

"We just got the call," I say.

"Write me something good," says Elvis.

"Write it right now," says the Colonel.

Mike and I go into a mixing room where there's an upright piano in the corner.

"You know what, Mike," I say. "Let's not screw around with anything overly inventive. Let's write this guy a straight-up, no-nonsense twelve-bar blues with a Christmas lyric. What do you say?"

"Okay by me."

I start singing:

> *Hang up your pretty stockings*
> *And turn off the light*
> *'Cause Santa Claus is coming down your chimney tonight*

It takes us about fifteen minutes. When we come back into the studio, I say, "Okay, we got it."

"What took you so long?" the Colonel asks.

"Writer's block," I say.

The Colonel doesn't laugh and the Colonel doesn't smile when we run down the song for Elvis. I know the Colonel thinks it's too bluesy and too black, but just before he can say anything, the King speaks out.

"Now that's what I call a goddamn great Christmas song!" he tells the Colonel. "I told you these guys would come through."

And with that, Elvis proceeds to sing the shit out of it.

He does it in just a couple of takes. When he's through, he puts his arms around me and Mike and says, "Whenever I record, you guys are gonna be with me."

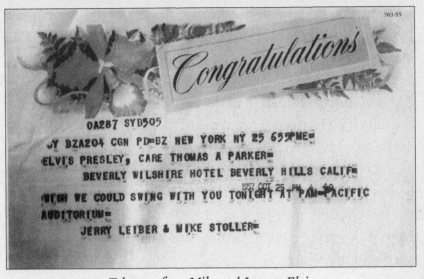

Telegram from Mike and Jerry to Elvis.

For me, "Santa Claus Is Back in Town" lives on as one of Elvis's great blues performances. It took him back to his Beale Street roots, a place where he was always comfortable.

Stoller Given Elvis's enthusiasm for our work, I wasn't surprised that we got a call from Jean Aberbach inviting us to his LA office, which was housed in a big home on Hollywood Boulevard.

"The Colonel wants to manage you," he said.

"We're unmanageable," Jerry was quick to retort. "Everyone knows that."

"This isn't a joke," Aberbach insisted.

"I wasn't joking," said Jerry. "We don't need management."

"Is that how you feel, Mike?" asked Aberbach.

"Absolutely."

"The Colonel feels he can do great things for your career," said Aberbach, "and he'd like you to sign these contracts." He handed us blank pieces of paper with only a signature line.

"Are you kidding?" we asked.

"No," Jean answered. "The Colonel said we can fill it in later, but basically it's a matter of mutual trust."

The Colonel got over our rejection of his offer. We knew that because we got a call late in 1957 that Elvis wanted more Leiber and Stoller songs. By then Jerry and I had made a permanent move to New York—more on that shortly—and went back to the Coast for a series of meetings.

The first was with Ben Hecht, the great Hollywood screenwriter, who had written, among many important works, *Notorious* for Alfred Hitchcock and *The Front Page*. Hecht had been in touch with us about an idea of Jerry's, a musical based on *Ali Baba and the Forty Thieves*. Despite the week we spent with him at his beach home in Oceanside, California, the project never materialized. Welcome to Hollywood.

The second reason we had returned to LA was Elvis. He wanted us to write songs for his new movie, *King Creole*. It was based on Harold Robbins's novel *A Stone for Danny Fisher*, and the screenplay suggested some real substance. We submitted four songs—"King Creole," "Trouble," "Steadfast, Loyal and True," and "Dirty Dirty Feeling." Elvis liked all four. ("Dirty Dirty Feeling" was dropped from the score, but two years later, when Elvis got out of the army, he remembered the tune and recorded it.) We worked in the studio with Elvis and, just like the *Jailhouse Rock* sessions, the rapport was good and the atmosphere relaxed. The Colonel may have been resentful that we turned down his offer for management, but when Elvis was happy—and whenever we were around, he seemed happy—the Colonel wasn't about to complain.

Colonel Parker and Elvis.

Leiber   I was in New York. It was a rainy winter night and I
found myself in a little cabaret. Cy Coleman, a wonderful pianist and
classy composer—he wrote "Witchcraft" for Sinatra and Broadway
shows like *Sweet Charity*—had hipped me to the place. The crowd
was showbizzy with a jazzlike edge. The chick singer that night also
had an edge. I ordered a double Maker's Mark and found a small
table by the bandstand. When she sang Cole Porter's "Let's Do It,"
I couldn't help but take it personally. She was looking right at me—
and real good. After her set she joined me.

   "I know who you are," she said.

"How?"

"I like the Coasters, I like Ruth Brown. And I love Big Mama Thornton. I look at the labels and notice the writers. Plus, Cy Coleman is crazy about you. He pointed you out last week."

"I'm flattered."

"I'm flattered that you stayed to hear me sing."

"It was a pleasure."

"Well, Jerry, it would give me pleasure if you hung around for another set and then let me take you to a very hot party over on the East Side. There'll be all sorts of people there."

"I like all sorts of people," I said.

"Then we're on."

"We sure as hell are."

As she sang her last set, I was in heaven. Nothing is more exciting than knowing—or at least believing—that you're going to get laid. Especially when you don't have to work for it. And on this stormy night, this gal was doing all the work.

After her last song was sung, she came to my table, took me by the arm, led me to the hatcheck girl, where she got my overcoat and Borsalino, slipped into her mink jacket, led the way to the street and hailed a cab. When we arrived at a swanky address on Sixty-second Street on the Upper East Side, she paid for the cab. Another bonus.

A white-gloved doorman directed us to the party in the penthouse. When the elevator door opened, I was about a foot away from Gary Cooper.

The singer winked at me.

"Welcome to the party," she whispered. "Have yourself a ball."

She was the kind of cool chick who could handle herself in such a glamorous setting. She wandered off her way and I wandered off mine. I tried not to gawk at Cary Grant and Claudette Colbert standing with drinks in their hands in front of a floor-to-ceiling window and chatting intimately, the neon city blazing below. If that was Marlene Dietrich on a loveseat in the living room, well, so be it.

I went to the bar and got another double bourbon. I examined the Cubist paintings on the walls.

"Jerry," said the singer who had found me. "I'd like you to meet Charlie Feldman."

Charlie Feldman was a big-time film producer.

"Glad to meet you, Leiber," he said. "I admire the work you and Stoller have done with Elvis."

"Thanks."

"In fact, I've been looking for you guys. It's providential that we're meeting here. Do you know Nelson Algren's *A Walk on the Wild Side*?"

"I think Algren's a great writer."

"Well, I think the book would make a great movie. I just bought the film rights. My idea is this—Elia Kazan directs, Budd Schulberg writes the adaptation, Elvis stars, and Leiber and Stoller write the score. What do you think?"

"I love it."

"Will you bring it to Elvis?"

"Gladly."

When I turned around to thank the singer for introducing me to Feldman, she was gone. I looked around. I caught a glimpse of her just leaving the party with Dietrich. She waved to me and said, "I hope it works out, Jerry."

"For you too, baby!" And with that, I blew her a kiss.

Stoller

When Jerry came back with the idea about Elvis in *A Walk on the Wild Side*, I flipped. It was a natural, a perfect vehicle for Elvis to expand his acting chops and a great opportunity for us to write a really hip score.

We set an appointment with Jean Aberbach and his brother Julian at their office in the Brill Building. We just knew how excited they'd be.

Jerry pitched the idea. "We're talking about a Kazan-Schulberg collaboration," he said, "the same team that did *On the Waterfront* for Brando. This is exactly the career move that will take Elvis to another level. He's a natural. He just needs brilliant material, a great director, and some real training."

"I'll have to speak to the Colonel about this, of course," said Jean. "I'll call him right away. Would you boys mind waiting outside for a few minutes?"

We waited for what seemed an eternity. We wondered what sort of reward or praise would be showered upon us for bringing in this fabulous prize. Finally, we were summoned back into the office.

Jean was stern when he said, "The Colonel has asked me to inform you that if you two ever try to interfere in the career of Elvis Presley again, you'll never work in Hollywood, New York, or anywhere else."

And with that, the project was over before it started. The Colonel had no interest in gambling on anything arty. His golden goose was going to lay the same egg, over and over. Don't mess with a proven formula.

Leiber

Despite our attempts to upgrade Elvis's film career, we were not banished. In fact, every time Elvis went into the studio we'd get a call from Bienstock or Jean Aberbach saying that the King wanted us there. Even though we always wanted to work with Elvis, there came a time when it wasn't possible.

I was walking down MacDougal Street in the Village when suddenly I passed out. A good Samaritan cab driver scooped me up off the street and tried to get me into a hospital, but five different ones turned him down until he finally found a place in Harlem willing to give me a bed. I was there for over a week. Turned out I had walking pneumonia. I was too weak to tell anyone what had happened. But as far as Mike knew, I had fallen off the face of the earth.

When I finally got back to my apartment on Washington Place, a pile of Western Union telegrams was waiting for me. All of them said, "Jerry, Elvis is going to record. You and Mike must fly to LA immediately. The Colonel."

I called Tom Parker and explained that I had just gotten out of the hospital. The Colonel said, "Some California sunshine is just what the doctor ordered."

"Well, Tom, I'd like to be there. I'll call my doctor and call you right back."

"Okay," said the Colonel, "I'll give you fifteen minutes."

I reached my doctor, who said, "Are you crazy? You can't leave your apartment for at least three weeks, and maybe not even then."

When I told this to Tom, he replied, "You know, Jerry, these doctors are full of shit. They treat us like babies. Look, I know you're going to be fine. Get on that plane, have a shot of bourbon, and get your ass out here. Hey, Mike's not sick, is he? Tell him to start packing."

I was thinking, *We're writing songs for the biggest star in the country, maybe the world, and they're begging us to write him more tunes and hang out in the studio with him. We could have hit after hit with Elvis. It was like an annuity, like hitting the jackpot every time. Should we screw it up and blow the whole deal?*

I called Mike and told him everything.

"Look, Mike," I said, "the doctor says I'm too weak to fly, but I hate to screw this deal up for us. The Colonel wants us to leave tonight. The Colonel is adamant. What should I tell him?"

Mike thought for a few minutes and then said, "Tell him to go fuck himself."

Stoller

The Colonel wrote us off, but Elvis didn't. He went on to cover many of our songs—"Girls, Girls, Girls" and "Little Egypt," which we wrote and produced for the Coasters; "Fools Fall in Love," first done by the Drifters; "Bossa Nova Baby," written for the Clovers; and "Saved," which LaVern Baker had recorded. Other than these covers, Elvis sang only one new song of ours, "She's Not You," which we wrote with Doc Pomus. That happened in 1962.

Our soul brother, Doc, had started out singing blues with jazz bands—another Jewish boy immersed in black culture. His partner, Mort Shuman, was twelve years younger. Mort was tall and thin, Doc short and wide. They were a gifted team and wrote dozens of hits, including "Viva Las Vegas" for Elvis. Eventually Mort became restless in New York and traveled to Mexico and Japan to expand his horizons. He wound up in Paris, where he became so fluent in French that the Parisians assumed he was a native. There he became an intimate of the great Belgian singer-songwriter Jacques Brel. He wrote English lyrics for a number of Brel's songs. He also co-produced and co-starred in *Jacques Brel Is Alive and Well and Living in Paris*. Mort's relocation left Doc alone. That's how Doc happened to call Jerry and me one day to propose that the three of us write something for Elvis. The result was "She's Not You" which, due to Doc's good relationship with the Aberbachs and the Colonel, Elvis recorded.

Meanwhile, back in the late fifties, Jerry and I started our first wholly-owned publishing company. As permanent residents of New York City, we were also part of the rhythm & blues and rock and roll revolution. Everything was changing, and we found ourselves, by sheer coincidence or exceptionally good fortune, smack dab in the middle of the action.

Girdles

Leiber   Our West Fifty-seventh Street office in Manhattan was on the top floor of a small building. On the street level was a store that featured women's foundation garments. That meant girdles, corsets, and other intimate items.

I liked watching the women who wandered into the store. I liked imagining what they looked like without their dresses. Some were portly, others shapely. Many didn't look like they needed girdles. Maybe they were shopping for their mothers. Whatever their consumer needs, the flow of female customers in and out of that establishment was endlessly intriguing. I liked the thought that while Mike and I were banging out ideas for songs, four stories below women were wiggling in and out of underwear. The images associated with girdle shopping were not unpleasant.

We were doing a Coasters session when Billy Guy happened to mention a song he'd heard on the radio about shopping. He recited as much of the lyric as he could remember, but he couldn't recall the name of the record or the singer. I loved the idea. I tried unsuccessfully to find the record. Still it was too good for the Coasters to pass up. So I assembled the lyric based upon what Billy remembered and Mike set it to music. Later we learned that a guy named Kent Harris wrote "Clothes Line," the song Billy had heard, and we eventually sorted out the credits—he became a co-writer. While it has nothing to do with women or girdles, the song does address the idea of shopping. And the subject matter is one of my favorites—fine men's clothes. We called it "Shoppin' for Clothes."

> *I was shopping for a suit the other day*
> *And walked into the department store*
> *Stepped on the elevator and told the girl*
> *"Dry goods floor"*
>
> *When I got off, a salesman come up to me*
> *He said, "Now, what can I do for you"*
> *I said, "Well, go in there and show me all them sport clothes*
> *Like you s'pposed to"*
>
> *He said, "Well, sure, come on in, buddy*
> *Dig these fabrics we got laid out on the shelf"*
> *He said, "Pick yourself out one*
> *Try it on, stand in the mirror and dig yourself"*

Stoller "Shoppin' for Clothes" is a story spoken over a sly funky beat with King Curtis's sensuous tenor sax providing the subtext. During live performances, the Coasters would roll out a clothing rack and dramatize the song as though it were a play.

When we settled in New York to stay, the Coasters were still our mainstay. The looser we got in the studio, the more fun we had, the more remarkable the results.

Back in 1957, Jerry and I had gone to record the Coasters at Chess Studios in Chicago, where the group was gigging. During that engagement, Bobby Nunn and Leon Hughes got a little out of hand, and manager Lester Sill replaced them. Will "Dub" Jones took Bobby's place and Cornell Gunter stepped in for Leon. The lineup of Billy Guy, Carl Gardner, Dub Jones, and Cornell Gunter did most of the great Coasters classics, including the aforementioned "Shoppin' for Clothes."

Another cutup and boisterous clown, Cornell became the protector of the group. He had an eighteen-inch neck and was strong as an ox. Once when an assailant went after one of his brother Coasters, Cornell grabbed the guy and threw him over a pickup truck. Yet you wouldn't exactly call Cornell macho. The minute he opened his mouth, you knew he was gay. He had queenly elocution and, in fact, did a dead-on imitation of the Queen of the Blues, Dinah Washington. (Listen to his lead vocal on "Easy Living" from the Coasters' *One by One* in which he transforms into Miss D herself. In fact, that LP not only features Cornell but demonstrates that Carl, Billy, and Dub were all capable singers of standards.)

Dub had one of the great bass voices. He was a deeply religious man with real heart and soul. Some bass singers have mere volume; but Dub had both resonance and subtlety. He was an artist.

In 1958, we developed a new approach to the Coasters' records. A duet lead featuring Carl and Billy. It all started with a song.

I was working with Jerry at his apartment. He was boiling water in the kitchen while I was fooling with some ideas on the piano. I hit on an especially happy rhythm pattern that I thought would fit the Coasters to a tee. As soon as Jerry heard it, he yelled from the kitchen, "Take out the papers and the trash!" Just like that, I yelled back, "Or you don't get no spending cash!" The tune just demanded two-part harmony; ten minutes later, "Yakety Yak" was born.

> *Take out the papers and the trash*
> *Or you don't get no spendin' cash*
> *If you don't scrub that kitchen floor*
> *You ain't gonna rock and roll no more*
> *Yakety yak (don't talk back)*

As soon as we recorded it, I knew it was a smash. Jerry wasn't so sure. He thought we needed some insurance by putting the old standard "Zing, Went the Strings of My Heart," on the flip side. I wanted to take a free ride by putting one of our own songs on the B-side, but Jerry won out.

Happily, "Yakety Yak" hit #1.

Leiber After "Yakety Yak," I thought we could write every Coasters hit in ten minutes. Man, was I wrong! When we tried to write a follow-up, Mike had lots of musical ideas, but I was stuck. I remember going to the Atlantic studio. Tommy Dowd, their brilliant engineer, was around. Tommy knew more about making records than Wexler and Ertegun combined, but he never got the credit. He was a great guy who inspired me with his wonderful musical instinct.

"It ain't coming, Tommy," I said, referring to the nonexistent follow-up to "Yakety Yak."

"It will," said Tommy, always a positive cat.

"When?"

"When it's ready."

It wasn't ready that day, or the next, or the day after. After nearly

"Charlie Brown" *sheet music.*

a week of agonizing, a simple name came to mind. "Charlie Brown." Then, "He's a clown, that Charlie Brown."

Mike already had a skip-along melodic template in place. He helped me with the story and suddenly a character, played by Dub Jones, stepped out on stage.

> *Fee fee, fi fi, fo fo, fum*
> *I smell smoke in the auditorium*
> *Charlie Brown, Charlie Brown*

He's a clown, that Charlie Brown
He's gonna get caught, just you wait and see
"Why is everybody always picking on me?"

Stoller
Jerry and I were at my place at 241 East Seventeenth Street. My first child, my daughter, Amy, was a newborn and I was in new-dad heaven. It was 1958. Jerry and I were discussing the follow-up to "Charlie Brown." As usual, our conversation veered off course and I began talking about the teacher I had back in Los Angeles, Arthur Lange, who had instructed me in composition. Lange had scored films, and one of them was called *Along Came Jones*, a 1945 Western with Gary Cooper and Loretta Young.

"Great title," said Jerry.

"Yeah, but it's been used already."

"Who cares? You can't copyright a title."

I plopped down in my easy chair and turned on Channel 2
A bad gunslinger called Salty Sam was chasin' poor Sweet Sue
He trapped her in the old sawmill and said with an evil laugh
"If you don't give me the deed to your ranch
    I'll saw you all in half"
And then he grabbed her—and then—
He tied her up—and then—
He turned on the buzzsaw—and then—and then—
And then along came Jones
Tall thin Jones
Slow walkin' Jones
Slow talkin' Jones
Along came long lean lanky Jones

The procedure for making a Coasters record went like this: Jerry performed the song and Billy or Carl copied Jerry's performance. I wrote out the charts and played piano. Jerry supervised from the booth. At first, I worked out the harmonies, but when Cornell came along, he took over that role.

A rehearsal with the Coasters was more like a party than work. When the guys came in off the road, they performed the choreography that they had created for the last batch of songs, and Jerry and I would be on the floor. Then we played them the new songs we had written for them, with Jerry acting out the stories, and they'd be rolling on the floor, howling.

The more we worked with the Coasters, the stronger the bond between us became. Even our culinary habits had a certain distinct harmony to them. There were, of course, four Coasters plus Jerry and myself. Billy Guy was living with a Jewish woman. I say that so you'll understand the order we phoned into the downstairs deli during a rehearsal:

three pastramis on rye with mustard
two pastramis on whole wheat with mayo
one pastrami on white bread with ketchup

The deli owner called back. "Is this some kind of joke?"

I explained that it wasn't; it was more a matter of ethnic diversity.

From then on, whenever we called in the pastrami order, the counter man would shout, "It's the Leiber and Stoller special!"

Leiber After "Along Came Jones" hit, we figured it was time to go back to something funky. That's how we came up with "I'm a Hog for You":

I'm a hog for you, baby
Can't get enough of your love
When I go to sleep at night
That's the only thing I'm dreamin' of

One little piggy went to London
One piggy went to Hong Kong
But this little piggy's comin' over your house
He's gonna rock you all night long

Stoller Back in the fifties, record companies didn't make single-song DJ copies. They sent out two-sided singles. Well, the B-side to "Hog" was another song that we recorded at the end of a Coasters session. We only had time for two takes before the three-hour session was up. We recorded it in time, but I saw it as a definite B-side. As right as I was about "Yakety Yak," that's how wrong I was about "Poison Ivy."

Leiber Pure and simple, "Poison Ivy" is a metaphor for a sexually transmitted disease—or the clap—hardly a topic for a song that hit the Top Ten in the spring of 1959. But the more we wrote, the less we understood why the public bought what it bought. It didn't make sense, but it didn't matter. We were having fun.

> She comes on like a rose
> But everybody knows
> She'll get you in Dutch
> You can look, but you better not touch
> Poison Ivy, Poison Ivy
> Late at night while you're sleepin'
> Poison Ivy comes a-creepin' around

Stoller The ultimate comic playlet for the Coasters was "Little Egypt," which wasn't a huge hit but, for me, along with "Along Came Jones," had the most interesting construction and some of Jerry's funniest lines.

I went and bought myself a ticket and I sat down in
the very first row
They pulled the curtain up and when they turned the
spotlight way down low
Little Egypt came out struttin' wearin' nuttin' but a
button and a bow
Singing, ying-yang, ying-yang, ying-yang, ying-yang

She had a ruby on her tummy and a diamond big as
Texas on her toe
She let her hair down and she did the hoochie-coochie
real slow
When she did her special number on a zebra skin I
thought she'd stop the show

Tommy Dowd slowed the tape down to half speed. I recorded over the last refrain so, played at normal speed, my voice was an octave higher. I sounded like one of the Chipmunks.

13

What's My Line?

Stoller   Today R&B and rock and roll are taken seriously as
art forms. When we started writing and producing, a two-line review
in *Cash Box* magazine was the most one could expect for a blues or
R&B record. As far as Jerry and I were concerned, the songs we were
writing might have a lifespan of a few months. They were cute, they
were appealing, they were seductive. Singers liked to sing them and
fans liked to listen to them. But we didn't expect longevity. These
tunes were written in an era when stratification of popular music was
absolute. At the top were giants like George Gershwin and Irving
Berlin. At the bottom were guys like us.

Nothing put this into context more clearly than our 1958 appearance on *What's My Line?*, the popular prime-time quiz show that
summarized cultural attitudes of the late fifties. The format was
simple: there was a celebrity panel consisting of Bennett Cerf, the
urbane publisher, Arlene Francis, the actress, and Dorothy Kilgallen,
the gossip columnist. Vincent Price, the actor, was a guest panelist.
The moderator was newsman John Daly. The panelists (sometimes
wearing blindfolds) had to guess the occupations of the guests.

The whole affair had a stiff formality about it. The men wore suits and bow ties; the women wore gowns. Daly spoke the King's English. The humor was crisp but restrained.

Leiber

I thought it'd be a hoot to appear on the show. Naturally none of the panelists knew us, so we were good candidates and passed the producers' audition with flying colors. The panelists were sharp and nailed our profession after four or five questions. Then something strange happened. Daly, a decent guy, started trumpeting our accomplishments.

"These men have been very successful," he told the panelists. "'Hound Dog' alone has sold some five million copies."

"That's no excuse," Dorothy Kilgallen quipped, expressing the highbrow view of the day—that rock and roll was trash.

"Why did you write something called 'Hound Dog'?" asked Bennett Cerf.

"Money," Kilgallen said before we had a chance to answer.

Before we left, nice-guy Daly congratulated us on our achievement but added, "I hope you have a chance to do more serious things in music."

"We plan to," I said.

Looking back at that moment, I ask myself, *Why did I say that?*

Was I merely embracing the general attitude of the day—that R&B and rock and roll were junk and that the age of Irving Berlin and great songs had passed?

14

Driftin' in the City

Leiber   The end of the fifties, the start of the sixties. Ike on his way out, Kennedy on his way in. Thanks to Elvis and a host of other white boys, rhythm & blues had morphed into rock and roll. I want to say that we really had nothing to do with that. I want to say that we made no calculated moves or calculated adjustments in the way we made music or, more specifically, records. At the time, I thought that was true, but looking back I see that wasn't so. Unconsciously, we were in the avant-garde of a movement that we didn't even know was a movement or had an avant-garde. We wrote bluesy tunes—rhythm-&-blues-based ballads and dance grooves—that blues lovers like Elvis transformed into rock and roll. We also wrote songs for black groups like the Coasters and the Clovers who, once doo-woppers, were now considered rock and rollers. In "Yakety Yak" we even wrote the words, "If you don't scrub that kitchen floor, you ain't gonna rock and roll no more." Maybe a critic could see rock and roll as R&B or deconstructed/reconstructed doo-wop. At the time, no one knew exactly what to call anything. (And the same may be true today.) Our mentors, the bosses at Atlantic, even began the Cat Label in an attempt to identify what some were labeling "cat music"—or rock and roll.

Stoller

It's confusing—all that categorizing and subcategorizing—but new musical forms that would prove enormously popular were being born. Jerry and I were part of that process. You might even call us midwives.

On the Presley LP *Elvis' Golden Records*, released in 1958, the liner notes called us "the Gilbert and Sullivan of rock and roll." On other LPs from this period, we were called the "Grandfathers of Rock and Roll." At the time, we were twenty-five.

More and more, we got to be comfortable in the studio making the sounds we wanted to hear. We did a lot of unconventional things in order to produce those unusual sounds. The Coasters were the ideal vocal actors to dramatize these scripts. They were their own singing repertory players performing with flair, wit, and artistic cunning. They were open to our craziness and we were open to theirs. Out of this intense musical marriage something new was created.

The Coasters expanded from four to five singers when Earl "Speedo" Carroll joined. Speedo, formerly of the Cadillacs, was mischievously sly; his off-the-wall humor and naughty-boy persona fit in perfectly. Interestingly enough, he kept his day job as the janitor at P.S. 87 in New York. He believed in job security. Shortly after Speedo became a Coaster, Cornell quit to begin a new group of Coasters of his own in Vegas.

In whatever configuration, the Coasters left a strong impression on pop music. Some called it post-doo-wop rhythm & blues. Some called it pop playlets. Some called it rock and roll. People called the

*The Coasters, from left, Carl Gardner, Earl "Speedo"
Carroll, Billy Guy, Will "Dub" Jones, 1960.*

Coasters' style of music all sorts of things. The truth is that today,
a half century later, I really don't know what to call it. And I really
don't care.

Leiber I cared about the New York nightlife. To take the
edge off our crazy work schedule, I haunted the midtown bars
where, starting in early evening, I sought the company of other cre-

ative lunatics who found comfort, not to mention sweet escape, in the form of good gin with a subtle hint of vermouth.

One of my favorite spots was Downey's on Eighth Avenue. It attracted theater people, a segment of the city's population that never failed to fascinate me—producers, directors, actors, and especially actresses. By six or seven, Downey's was packed and, on any given evening in the late fifties, you'd see me at the bar, carrying on about this topic or that.

On this particular night, I was with my buddy Ben Gazzara. Ben was a raconteur. He'd achieved great acclaim on Broadway for his role as Brick in Tennessee Williams's *Cat on a Hot Tin Roof*, directed by Elia Kazan. He was pissed that Paul Newman got the role of Brick in the film. Barbara Bel Geddes, who'd done the female lead on stage, was replaced in the movie by Elizabeth Taylor. At the same time, though, Ben was happy because Otto Preminger cast him in his upcoming film *Anatomy of a Murder*. We were both excited that Preminger had commissioned Duke Ellington to do the score. Meanwhile, I was still bemoaning Colonel Parker's rejection of the Kazan-Schulberg-Leiber-Stoller and Elvis project.

The bullshit was flying fast and furiously when I noticed a beautiful woman walk in the bar in the company of a man. "Beautiful" is not quite enough. Stunning. Breathtaking. Heart-stopping.

I couldn't stop staring.

"That's Gaby Rodgers," said Gazzara. "She was in that film Mickey Spillane wrote, *Kiss Me Deadly*. The dame's drop-dead gorgeous. And her date is even prettier."

Miss Rodgers's companion, a big masculine guy, heard Ben but paid no attention. He and Miss Rodgers found a booth, where they were joined by two guys who seemed effeminate in the extreme. After a few minutes, the big man got up and made his way to our table. Suddenly I recognized him as Edward Mulhare, the Irish actor who had just replaced Rex Harrison in Lerner and Loewe's smash hit *My Fair Lady.*

"Gentlemen," he said to us, "and don't forget, I'm taking a liberty. When I walked by before, I hope I didn't hear someone refer to me as 'pretty.' I would have to take this as a homophobic remark. The homosexual friends with whom I'm dining tonight would be wounded by such a disparaging comment and I'd feel obliged to uphold their honor by solidly thrashing anyone who dared to be so insulting."

Mulhare had an enormous physical presence. For all his smooth sentence structure, his speech revealed a dangerous impatience.

"Apologies will be in order," he said, glaring directly into Ben's eyes.

No pushover himself, Ben glared back and then, after studying the size of Mulhare's hands, recanted. "I do apologize," said Gazzara reluctantly.

"I do accept," said Mulhare.

He excused himself and returned to the table with Miss Rodgers and the two other gentlemen.

That should have been that. But it wasn't. I couldn't keep my eyes off Miss Rodgers. And the more I drank, the more I stared. After three or four stiff ones, it didn't matter to me whether she was with Mulhare, the gay boys, or the Russian army. This woman was too good to be true.

I waited until Mulhare went to the bathroom before I made my move. Looking back, it wasn't much of a move, but it was completely sincere. I went over to her booth.

"I'm going to marry you," I said, staring directly into her eyes.

"And you're crazy," she said.

"Yes," I agreed. "But I'm still going to marry you."

Then I returned to my table and told Gazzara what I had told her.

"Invite me to the wedding," he said.

"Not if you behave like you've behaved tonight," I said.

"Fuck my behavior. If it wasn't for me, you wouldn't even know who she is."

"I know who she is. And who she's gonna be. She's gonna be my wife."

"And when do you plan to see her again?"

"Tomorrow night."

"Where?" asked Ben.

"Here," I said. "Right here."

Tomorrow night came and I was back at Downey's. So was Gaby Rodgers. This time she arrived with another actor. They went to the bar. I wasted no time in accosting her.

"Ah, it's the crazy man," she said.

"Ah, it's the movie star," I said.

"Hardly," she said.

Ironically, her date knew who I was. "This guy writes for Elvis. He's the hottest songwriter around," he told Gaby before he excused himself to call his agent. "This is the man who invented rock and roll."

"Hardly," I said.

Gaby smiled.

"Tell me about your rock and roll," she said.

"Tell me about your movie stardom," I said.

"Rock and roll is more interesting," she insisted.

"If only I knew anything about it."

"How could you not if you invented it?"

"Your friend is too kind."

"He says you're Elvis Presley's songwriter."

"My partner and I have written a few songs that Elvis has sung. That's all."

"You're being modest," Gaby said.

"If I am, it's a first. No one's ever accused me of that before."

"When it comes to men," Gaby added, "I'm not always the best judge."

"When it comes to female beauty, I am the best judge," I quipped. "And my summary judgment in your case is absolute. You are guilty of flawless beauty."

Gaby laughed out loud and said, "Such bullshit!"

"Bullshit is my business," I explained.

"Then you must be very successful," she said.

"Moderately. But everyone has different views of success. My view of success would be taking you to dinner."

"I'm not sure."

"I am. When can I see you again?"

"Who knows?"

And with that she was gone.

Stoller My personal life in New York was quite different from Jerry's. By the early sixties, Meryl and I had three beautiful children. After Amy came our sons, Peter and Adam. My relationship with Meryl was far from ideal. With increasing clarity I came to understand that my motivation for this early marriage was largely to escape my troubled home. There were tremendous compatibility problems between myself and Meryl, but for the sake of our kids, whom we both adored, we hung in and tried to create a relatively calm domestic life for ourselves in our place on Seventeenth Street.

My workroom on the top floor of our brownstone was a refuge from some of those marital conflicts I wasn't ready to address. I had regrown a goatee and adopted the affectation of carrying a tightly rolled umbrella wherever I went, rain or shine.

I also started studying with the twelve-tone composer Stefan Wolpe. He taught me a great deal, even though most of my pieces were emulations of his work. I wrote a quartet for flute, bass clarinet, harp, and cello where the meter changed every measure and the melody was filled with 64th and 128th notes, trademarks of the avant-garde. The composition was performed by a group of fine musicians at the 92nd Street Y, where the harpist completely blacked out in the second movement. I could hardly blame her.

Avant-garde music fascinated me. I loved much of it. But, in truth, I couldn't emotionally relate to my own piece.

It's strange, but if you asked either Jerry or me about what we were writing, we would have expressed pride. We knew our stuff was good, and we knew it was selling. Yet at the same time, we held in highest respect the undisputed masters: Lerner and Loewe, Rodgers and Hammerstein, Cole Porter, the Gershwins, and all the rest. In the back of our minds, we wanted to write musicals. We liked the idea of writing a collection of songs illustrating a dramatic story. But no one was asking us to do that.

Leiber The truth is that back then I was more interested in the pursuit of the fair Miss Rodgers than I was in writing a Broadway show. Night after night I saw her at Downey's. And night after night I pleaded my case.

"Because you're a lyricist," she said, "I see you as more talk than action."

"How can I prove you wrong?"

"I'm going to a production at the Bucks County Playhouse this weekend. I could use a ride."

"I'm your man."

"Do you have a car?"

"I have a sports car. It's recently waxed and at your disposal."

"How you do feel about the plays of Eugene Ionesco?"

"They're absurd. I'm absurd. I relate."

"Then don't be late. We leave tomorrow at noon."

I arrived early. It was early autumn, the weather was mild and the top was down. The talk was delicious. Gaby was far more cultural than I was. She spoke of the novels of Nabokov, the philosophy of Nietzsche, and the cantos of Ezra Pound, all with great naturalness and not a modicum of pretense. She adored good books and edgy art. She was conversant with challenging ideas and, best of all, she appreciated, as did I, how healthy quantities of booze helped fuel such conversations.

That weekend was splendid. As the great jazz ballad put it, I surrendered, "Body and Soul."

Stoller Jerry had always been an avid reader, but suddenly I noticed he was spending more and more time at art galleries and avant-garde theater. One night he came to our house on Seventeenth Street with an attractive lady whom he introduced as Gaby Rodgers. She and Jerry had, apparently, been seeing each other for a number of months. I intuited that she was the impetus behind his new intellectual pursuits. Jerry told me that he had been attending the Actors Studio with Gaby. His interest was in observing the work of various directors and drama theorists.

Leiber

It was a simple question that I asked Gaby.

"Is that a Cézanne over the fireplace?"

"Yes, it is," she said.

After a year of going out with me, Gaby got up the nerve to introduce me to her parents, who lived in a swanky Old World building on Central Park West. By then we were engaged and, like it or not, I had to meet my prospective in-laws.

Her mom, Lisa Latta, came from big-time European textile money. She was a tough battleaxe who had no use for me.

Her dad, Saemy Rosenberg, sipped cognac and sat in the corner of their enormous sitting room with its heavy drapes and Regency chairs. Mr. Rosenberg was one of the most important art dealers in the world. He sold the Metropolitan Museum of Art a great deal of its antique furniture. Gaby had told me that he'd recently sold the Cleveland Museum of Art a Rembrandt worth $10 million.

The four of us sat there, drinks in hand, not quite knowing what to say.

I wanted to discuss Gaby's recent role in *Juno and the Paycock*, the Sean O'Casey play. I was proud of the brilliant job she had done. But her mother was more interested in my name.

"How do you spell 'Leiber'?" she asked.

I told her.

I explained that was my father's spelling.

"And why did he choose that spelling as opposed to Lieber or Libber or Lubber? They have entirely different connotations."

"Mother," said Gaby, "why are you being difficult?"

"I'm not being difficult at all, my dear. I'm merely saying that the unorthodox spelling—or better yet, the *incorrect* spelling—leaves me perplexed. Why should a man carry a name that's a mistake?"

The conversation continued along this painful path until the old

Jerry and Gaby's wedding day.

man, much to his credit, interrupted his wife by saying, "For God's sake, Lisa, his name's Leiber because the idiots on Ellis Island spelled it that way. If they knew how to spell, they wouldn't be working at Ellis Island. Now that's enough."

From that moment on, I had a warm spot in my heart for Saemy Rosenberg, a man of culture and empathy.

Despite her mother's disapproval, Gaby and I were married in a civil ceremony in 1958. On the way down to city hall, her mother kept grilling me. Her questions always concerned my lineage. Where was my father born? My mother? And why didn't my mother come in for the wedding?

Of course, my mother and Mrs. Rosenberg would have wound up in a verbal mud wrestling match. But that wasn't something I could tell Gaby's mom.

"Mom's eager to meet Gaby," I said, "but it's a long trip from California."

"You'd think it's a trip she'd want to make," said my soon-to-be mother-in-law.

I kept quiet.

In the judge's chambers, we were joined by Robert Motherwell, the great painter, and his wife, Helen Frankenthaler, the equally great painter, our best man and best woman. These were friends I had met through Gaby.

At the wedding breakfast at the Colony Restaurant, my father-in-law ordered huge trays with mounds of Beluga caviar and bottles of 1949 Krug champagne.

By the end of the fifties, I was a twenty-seven-year-old man married to a woman who was certainly my soul mate. The problem was, I had a restless soul.

There Goes My Baby

Stoller At the end of the fifties and start of the sixties, Jerry and I started introducing new elements into our records. We weren't radicals with an agenda, just two guys fascinated with certain colors and rhythms.

We loved using different percussion instruments. Latin grooves, for example, had always fascinated me. As a kid in New York, I'd hang out in Spanish Harlem on hot summer afternoons with my buddy Al Levitt and our Puerto Rican girlfriends, listening to all-percussion jam sessions exploding from a brownstone building at 108th and Madison. The outside steps, or stoops as we called them in New York, became a bandstand—congas on the bottom step, bongos on the next step, and timbales, guiros, and cowbells on the step above. The echo down the canyon of the city's streets was fantastic. Moving to LA for my last semester of high school, I was exposed to another and different world of Latin rhythms.

As songwriters in New York, Jerry and I had fallen deeply in love with a Brazilian *baion* rhythm emanating from the northeastern province of Brazil called Bahia. We'd first heard the groove in the Italian film *Anna*. To create the groove in the studio, we'd go to Carroll's Broadway music store and rent whatever struck our fancy—tom-toms, congas, marimbas, triangles, and a monster we called the African hairy drum. We brought all this to bear when we began working with the Drifters.

Leiber In the mid-fifties, the Drifters were the preeminent vocal group in black music. The Drifters had been fronted by Clyde McPhatter who, along with Ray Charles, Sam Cooke, and Little Wil-

lie John, was one of the great soul singers of his generation. Clyde left Billy Ward & the Dominoes when Ahmet signed him and encouraged him to form a group of his own. Thus, in 1953, the Drifters were born. Great hits like "Money Honey" and "Honey Love" quickly followed. Then Clyde left the group. Atlantic kept them on the roster with a variety of singers, including Johnny Moore, who sang lead on "Fools Fall in Love." George Treadwell, a former trumpet player and ex-husband of Sarah Vaughan, managed the Drifters. Along with a couple of partners, he did more than manage; he owned the name and, in essence, owned the group itself. From then on, the actual Drifters were salaried employees. Not only did they *not* share in record royalties, their salaries covered their time for both recording *and* performing. As a result, the personnel changes were nonstop.

For an extended period in the late fifties, the Drifters went hitless. "It's a valuable name," Jerry Wexler told George Treadwell. "It's a commercial name. Find some new Drifters so we can cut some sides and make some money." Treadwell found the Crowns, whose lead singer was Ben E. King. The Crowns became the Drifters.

"You've been doing so well with the Coasters," Wexler told us, "that we're entrusting you with one of our most important acts—the Drifters. Just don't go over budget. Keep it simple."

Stoller We did anything but keep it simple. As the guys were rehearsing, I started playing a Borodin-like counterline on the piano. Jerry said, "That sounds like strings." I said, "Hey, why not?"

We worked it up, and then we worked it up some more. I gave my counterline to Stan Applebaum, a wonderful orchestrator whose contributions to Leiber-Stoller productions were considerable. On "There Goes My Baby," Stan used my line and added some lines of his own, scoring it for four violins and a cello. The five strings augmented our basic R&B rhythm section. We noticed a kettle drum in the corner of the studio. Our drummer had never played any timpani before and couldn't figure out how to use the foot pedal to change the pitch. Throughout four chords, he could play only the same pitch over and over, creating a kind of harmonic mud. Then, of course, the *baion* beat was bringing everything to a boil.

So suddenly the song was all over the place. With the Drifters' soaring vocals, Applebaum's soaring orchestration, and the studio's heavy echo, there was an awful lot going on. But we were convinced that it worked.

Leiber I was convinced it was a smash hit and couldn't wait to play it for Wexler and Ahmet, who had not been in the studio when we produced it. After one listen, Wexler turned to me and pronounced it dead. "I'd never release shit like this," he said. "It's dog meat. You've wasted our money on an overpriced production that sounds like a radio caught between two stations. It's a goddamn awful mess!" As he said it, Wexler was spitting his tuna fish sandwich against the wall. *Splat!* It stuck.

Stoller Wexler's opinion didn't really faze us. We were sure of ourselves.

Ahmet didn't care for it any more than Wexler did, but, always the diplomat, he said, "We know you boys make great records, but you can't hit a home run every time." At our request, he allowed us two hours with Tommy Dowd to remix the song.

2LEIBER & STOLLER

160

The mix came out brilliantly, but Wexler, ever the bull, still hated it and refused to put it out for the longest time. We kept protesting, but to no avail.

Leiber Atlantic finally released "There Goes My Baby." The result was immediate and dramatic. "There Goes My Baby" was an instant smash. It hit #1, sold over a million copies, and was declared one of the most important records in the annals of the great Atlantic label. The long-dormant Drifters were back in business. In fact, manager George Treadwell decided to expand the franchise. If he could hire four Drifters, he could just as easily hire twelve. And that's what he did: he had one set of Drifters performing in New York, another in LA, and a third in Cleveland. They were all singing "There Goes My Baby."

Meanwhile, our credentials as producers shot through the roof. We couldn't wait to go back into the studio. Before that, though, we made another move. We got new offices. This doesn't sound like any big deal, and at the time we didn't think twice about it. We had felt a little isolated on Fifty-seventh Street above the girdle shop. We wanted to be around other songwriters and song publishers. We decided to rent space in a building at Forty-ninth and Broadway.

The Brill Building

Stoller It was 1961, and we were where we wanted to be. As a kid in the forties when I looked at sheet music, I never failed to see that every song had a publisher located at 1619 Broadway.

Leiber You'd go to the men's room on the ninth floor of the Brill Building. You'd open the door and suddenly the sound of four-part harmony would hit you in the face. A vocal group was rehearsing by the toilets because the sound bouncing off the tile created this groovy echo. In the Brill Building, even the bathrooms overflowed with musical inspiration.

You'd leave the bathroom and walk back to your office. Right next door you'd see Irving Caesar, the same Irving Caesar who wrote "Tea for Two," not to mention "Swanee" with George Gershwin.

"Where you going, Irving?" you'd ask.

"I'm going to the track. Where else would I be going?"

Mike and Jerry on the terrace of the Brill Building.

Every day, along with half the guys in the Brill Building, Irving Caesar went to the track.

Stoller The Brill Building was old school, new school, and every school mixed together. At one time the building was almost exclusively occupied by old-time songwriters, music publishers, bandleaders, and agents.

Up the street, 1650 Broadway was just as musical as the Brill Building. Sixteen-fifty had a full recording studio in the basement and a demo studio on the ninth floor where you'd see everyone from Neil Diamond to Neil Sedaka.

Next to our office in the Brill Building was Ed Burton, who'd signed a singer-songwriter named Bobby Darin. Before long, Ed was working for Bobby.

Publishers had offices with cubicles barely big enough to house the upright pianos on which songwriters banged out their ideas fast and furiously. The publishers employed song pluggers whose job was to get singers and bands to record their songs. The building was overrun by hustlers, some genuinely gifted, others genuinely jive. Every day a writer or two would start on the eleventh floor and bang on the door of every single publisher. If he were let in, he'd take out his accordion or just tap his foot and sing his song. Guys like "Run Joe" Taylor were sometimes lucky enough to sell a song for ten or twenty bucks, and then keep going and sell the same song again to another publisher. Rumor had it that one genius, working both the Brill and 1650 Broadway, sold the same song no fewer than fourteen times in a single day.

But the big picture, of course, is that the old school—the Irving Caesars—was dying out and a new school was being born. That new school would be represented by hot young writers like Jeff Barry, Ellie Greenwich, Doc Pomus, and Morty Shuman at 1619; and over at 1650, Carole King, Gerry Goffin, Barry Mann, and Cynthia Weil, just to name the most famous. Other than Doc, they were younger than us. If we were twenty-seven, they were barely out of their teens. They looked up to us as the crazy guys who pulled off "There Goes My Baby." We admired their spirit and energy and feel for a new kind of R&B/rock and roll that was centered, to a large degree, on the sensibilities of teenagers. The age of the girl group, another major phenomenon in pop music, was dawning, and we found ourselves surrounded by writers who understood the teen heart and mind.

Leiber While we were working with groups like the Drifters and immersing ourselves in the pop culture of the day, we were also offered a project that threw us into the world of avant-garde music.

Stoller Jerry and Gaby were living in a brownstone on East Seventy-second Street where their neighbor was producer George Justin. Justin was doing *Something Wild*, a movie with Carroll Baker, who had made her name starring in the Elia Kazan–Tennessee Williams film *Baby Doll*. Baker's husband, Jack Garfein, was the screenwriter and director of this new film, while Morton Feldman, the avant-garde composer, was writing the background score. Justin wanted to know if Jerry and I were interested in writing the theme. We were.

Feldman was an intriguing choice, and we saw the assignment as a creative challenge. Things got especially challenging when we met with Morty before the recording session. I'd written a jazz theme and a big band arrangement, Jerry had written a lyric and we'd put together an orchestra of great musicians, half from the Basie band and half from Ellington's.

"I have an idea," Morty told me. "Let me take your arrangement and redistribute it into various small groups. Then you, Jerry, and I will each conduct the ensembles at different tempos, all at the same time and in the same studio. What do you say, Mike?"

"Why not?"

Jerry was game and we were off and running. The result was annoying, frightening, and wonderfully nauseating. It would have worked phenomenally well in the film.

Then came the poisonous phone call from George Justin. Jack Garfein decided that his film was a masterpiece. He threw out the Morton Feldman score and the Leiber and Stoller theme and replaced us with Aaron Copland!

Naturally, I was disappointed, but it was all worthwhile because it forged my friendship with Morty Feldman. Morty was a truly original character. When I became interested in writing for the harp, it was Morty who introduced me to Carlos Salzedo, the great virtuoso. For reasons I would understand only later, I kept hearing harp music in my head and wanted to know more about the instrument. "Salzedo is your man," said Morty. "He'll answer all your questions."

Morty and I trudged over to Salzedo's Riverside Drive apartment in the midst of a ferocious snowstorm. Carlos could not have been more forthcoming, and I gained invaluable insight into the harp and its infinite possibilities. When we left, the storm had become a blizzard. Snowdrifts were three feet high.

"Let's duck in a restaurant and get something to eat," I said.

"Yes," said Morty, "I'm starved."

"How about Chinese?" I asked, pointing to a place on the corner.

We fought the storm and managed to walk over there.

"We can't eat here," said Morty.

"Why not?"

"I can't eat in a Chinese restaurant that's not a walk-up. I can't eat on the ground floor."

Through the blowing snow I saw another Chinese place two doors down that was a walk-up. But when we made it up the stairs, Morty wouldn't go inside.

"What's wrong?" I asked.

"They don't have a handwritten menu. I can't eat Chinese food in a restaurant that doesn't have a handwritten menu."

A half hour later, both of us half-frozen, we found still another chop suey joint that was both upstairs and presented us with a menu written in longhand. The food wasn't great, but Morty was happy.

Morty introduced me to John Cage and Merce Cunningham as well as his many painter friends. Morty's music was soft, ranging from *p* to *ppppp*, usually performed at extremely to impossibly slow tempos. He said that his music was influenced by the abstract expressionist painters. Through Morty I met Robert Rauschenberg, Larry Rivers (who had played baritone sax in Boyd Raeburn's big band), Philip Guston, and Howard Kanovitz, a former trombonist with Gene Krupa, soon to be my fishing buddy and one of my dearest friends. One of my funniest memories was a jam session at a roadhouse bar in Jackson Pollock's old East Hampton neighborhood where Larry, Howard, and I, fueled by whiskey and wine, played all night long.

17

He Wore
His Ambition
Like a Topcoat

Leiber   Let me tell you about another character. This all
started in 1960, even before we moved into the Brill Building.

One day I answered the phone.

"Jerry, it's Lester."

"How are you, Lester?"

I was always happy to hear from Lester Sill, our mentor, the
Coasters' manager, and the guy who believed in us from the get-go.
He was calling from LA. We were still in our Fifty-seventh Street
office. "I'm fine, Jer, but I have a favor to ask."

"Shoot."

"I have a kid here. A kid I believe in. I believe in him the way I
believed in you and Mike. In fact, he's another Leiber and Stoller. He
comes from New York but moved to LA and went to Fairfax High.
He's an R&B genius, a guitarist, a writer, an arranger, a producer.
And he idolizes you, Jer. I swear he does."

"What's his name?"

"Phil Spector. Ever hear of him?"

"No."

"Well, he talks about you, Jer, like you're the pope."

"Bless him. What does he want?"

"To come to New York."

"Fine. Have him come to New York."

"But he needs a ticket."

"He doesn't have money for a plane ticket?"

"No."

"And you want me to pay?"

"As a favor to me, Jer. You won't regret it. He already has a hit with the Teddy Bears. 'To Know Him Is to Love Him.'"

"And you love him, Lester?" I asked.

"You will too."

I didn't.

A week later Phil Spector arrived on our dime. He came directly from the airport to our office and asked if he could sleep on the couch. What could we say? It didn't matter that he forgot to thank me for the ticket or that he was an annoying presence. I had the feeling he was smart. I definitely knew he loved music, and he wore his ambition like a topcoat; it was all over him.

Stoller   We signed Phil to an exclusive publishing contract, giving him a monthly advance that, admittedly, wasn't a whole lot. To augment his income, though, we put him on all our sessions. By that time we were using four guitars on most of our dates and Phil became the fifth.

Leiber

Phil was like a puppy dog, except he wasn't especially loveable. Everywhere I went, he wanted to follow. He had this terrific fear of abandonment. He was frightened to death of being left alone. He said that was because his father had committed suicide. He told me a story about being on the road with the Teddy Bears. They were in some small town in Texas. Phil went to the bathroom and four guys, thinking he was strange, followed him in. They pushed him against the wall and pissed all over him. That's another reason he gave for not being able to be alone—ever. I felt sorry for the guy, and I felt indebted to Lester Sill, so once he couldn't stand sleeping in our office anymore, I let him live in my house. At our sessions, he watched us like a hawk—the instrumentation we used, the multiple percussionists playing the *baion* rhythm pattern, our method of mixing, the whole shmear.

Phil hung around, hoping to pick up whatever scraps might come his way. He bugged us to let him produce. When we were asked to go in the studio with the singer Ray Peterson for Big Top Records, I convinced them to let Phil do the job. Mike and I guaranteed his work. One of the songs he did was Ray Peterson's hit cover of "Corinna, Corinna," the tune Big Joe Turner had made famous.

Phil produced a "Corinna" Lite—a bloodless redo of the original. Bloodless or not, the Spector-Peterson version went Top Ten. But the production gig wasn't enough. Phil kept asking the same question over and again, "When are we going to write together, Jerry?"

"I write with Mike," I said.

"Then Mike can write with us, too."

"You don't get it, Phil," I said. "If it happens, it isn't that Mike gets to write with you and me—it's that *you* get to write with me and Mike."

"That's what I meant, Jerry."

I asked Mike how he felt about writing with Phil.

"If you think it's a good idea," he said, "I'm game."

"Let's give it a try, Mike," I said, "if only to get this guy off my back."

We set an early evening date at my place.

Phil arrived early. Mike called to say he'd be late. Mike had been working such late hours that he hadn't seen much of his kids and had promised to have dinner with them that night.

Phil didn't want to wait for Mike and broke out his guitar. I'd been listening to Debussy's *Iberia* and Ravel's *Rhapsodie Espagnole* and suggested we do something with a Spanish feel. Phil liked the idea and started strumming. Rather than set the story in Europe, I thought it would be interesting to set it in Harlem. The words came quickly to me:

> *There is a rose in Spanish Harlem*
> *A red rose up in Spanish Harlem*
> *It is a special one, it's never seen the sun*
> *It only comes out when the moon is on the run*
> *And all the stars are gleaming*
> *It's growing in the street, right up through the concrete*
> *But soft and sweet and dreaming*

Phil's melody had the right flavor and, before we knew it, the song was written.

When Mike called, I had to tell him that the song was already finished.

Stoller The next day I met Jerry and Phil at the conference room at Atlantic. They wanted to play the song for Ahmet,

Wexler, and me. Phil played the guitar and Jerry sang. I was sitting at the piano and started to play a fill between the phrases. The fill fit perfectly. When I worked on the arrangement, I wanted that figure to be played on the marimba. Since then, I've never heard the song played without that musical figure. I presumed my contribution was seminal to the composition, but I also knew that Phil didn't want to share credit with anyone but Jerry, so I kept quiet.

Jerry and I produced the record. It was one of the first four sides we produced with Ben E. King after he left the Drifters. Understand-

Ben E. King.

ably, Ben was sick and tired of being George Treadwell's indentured servant. We were happy to help him go solo.

I worked closely with arranger Stan Applebaum on the orchestration for "Spanish Harlem," laying out the marimba and curved soprano sax sections in the instrumental breaks. As always, Stan wrote fabulous string parts.

Around this same time, I remember arriving at our office as Jerry and Ben were working on lyrics for a new song. King had the beginnings of a melody that he was singing a cappella. I went to the piano and worked up the harmonies, developing a bass pattern that became the signature of the song. Ben and Jerry quickly finished the lyrics:

When the night has come
And the land is dark
And the moon is the only light we'll see
No, I won't be afraid, no, I won't be afraid
Just as long as you stand, stand by me

Leiber Years later, after "Stand by Me" was a #1 R&B smash, after it was a Top Five pop hit, after it had been covered by everyone and his mother, after Rob Reiner had made a hit movie using the title and featuring the song, a journalist asked me what made it so popular.

"Mike's bass line," I said.

"There's got to be more to it than that. What about the lyrics? The vocal?"

"The lyrics are good, King's vocal is great. But Mike's bass line pushed the song into the land of immortality. Believe me—it's the bass line."

Both of these songs we produced for King, "Spanish Harlem"

and "Stand by Me," required going overtime in the recording studio by thirty minutes with a large orchestra. The overtime incurred Wexler's wrath. But of course his wrath was assuaged when the two songs established Ben E. King as a solo artist of the first rank.

Stoller   Our skirmishes with Wexler didn't end there.

Barry Mann and Cynthia Weil brought us a tune for the Drifters called "Only in America." We liked it. It protested the indignities that blacks faced "only in America." Remember, this was 1963 and, rather than make it a blatant protest song, we decided the song could be even more effective as a satire with an obvious dose of irony. So Cynthia and Jerry reworked the lyric:

> *Only in America*
> *Can a guy from anywhere*
> *Go to sleep a pauper*
> *And wake up a millionaire*

We produced the song with the Drifters on the same day that Martin Luther King, Jr., was thrown into jail in Birmingham for staging a nonviolent demonstration in defiance of a court injunction.

Leiber   When Wexler heard it, he didn't like it. And, true to his style, he didn't beat around the bush.

"Leiber," he said to me, "are you nuts? They'll string us up by our balls."

"Who?" I asked.

"The militants. The militants are coming on strong and they'll see this as hogwash."

"I don't agree. The irony's too thick to be misunderstood."

"I'm not releasing it."

"Hey, if you're worried about the cost of making this track, maybe United Artists will buy it and we'll overdub another group."

"Great," said Wexler. "Sell it."

A year earlier, in 1962, Mike and I had scored a hit on United Artists with a white group called Jay and the Americans. The song was "She Cried." Given their name, we figured Jay and his boys would have no problems with "Only in America." So we took the Drifters off and put the Americans on. It changed from a satirical social protest song into a flag-waving piece of patriotism. And wouldn't you know it—the damn thing took off like a rocket.

Stoller By the way, now that Barack Obama is our president, those lyrics sung by a black singer don't seem as farfetched as they did in 1963:

> Only in America
> Can a kid without a cent
> Get a break and maybe grow up to be president

Leiber Wexler had a love-hate relationship with us. He admired our work but was always competitive. Yet we never felt competitive with him. He and Ahmet made great records, and we were happy to be hooked up with them. But seeing Spector as the new golden boy, Wexler started giving more plum production assignments to Phil and fewer to us.

Meanwhile, though, Phil had become enamored of Ahmet. In fact, he began imitating Ahmet's style of speaking. Ahmet was the suave hipster Spector longed to become. Ahmet saw Phil as a talented newcomer who had his finger on the pulse of teenage pop.

We knew Spector had talent, but we didn't trust him. Once Phil drifted over to Atlantic and began working for Ahmet and Wexler, we weren't surprised to learn that he didn't have the least interest in honoring that contract he had signed with us. Even more alarming was the fact that the contract was somehow missing. Someone apparently removed from our files that binding agreement giving us the publishing rights to whatever Spector wrote. It didn't take Dick Tracy to figure out who it might have been.

We let it go. To pursue Spector legally was more trouble than it was worth—at least that's what we thought at the time. Even worse, it would mean having more contact with Phil. As it happened, Spector never cut a single hit for Atlantic. Even more to the point, in spite of our bankrolling and promoting his career, besides "Spanish Harlem," he never wrote a hit song for us.

Stoller By watching us in the studio, Phil developed many of his production ideas. I have no regrets about that. Musical techniques are meant to be passed on and mutated. But it's annoying to hear Phil claiming credit for our productions. He did, in fact, play guitar on a few of those dates, but for most of those sessions he wasn't even in the studio.

After Phil's brief and uneventful time with Atlantic, he moved back to LA, where he started a company with our old mentor, Lester Sill, in 1961. They named it after themselves—Philles Records—and had an amazing run of hits by the Crystals, the Ronettes, Darlene Love, and others. By then Phil had developed what he called his Wall of Sound. The difference, though, between Spector's production approach and ours was this: While we went for instrumental clarity, Spector went for a sound that was anything but clear.

Many of these hits were written by Jeff Barry and Ellie Greenwich, writers signed to Trio Music Co., our publishing firm. The songs were credited to Barry-Greenwich-Spector, which meant once

From left, Jeff Barry, Phil Spector, Paul Case, Ellie Greenwich, and Jerry during the sixties.

again we had to deal with Phil. It wasn't easy, but we managed. Lester Sill wasn't as fortunate. Phil squeezed him out, and Philles Records became Phil's sole property in 1962.

Leiber I remember sitting in my office in the Brill Building when a short, well-dressed black man came in to see us. He introduced himself as Berry Gordy. He reminded us that he had co-written hits for Jackie Wilson like "Lonely Teardrops," "I'll Be Satisfied," and "Reet Petite."

He described his dream. He wanted to make R&B more appealing to whites by softening the sound. He brought along some songs and tapes. I listened carefully.

"What do you think?" he asked me.

"The material is okay," I said. "Some of it is good."

"Then you'll help me," he assumed.

"No."

"Why not?" he asked.

"Because you don't need me. You can identify and sign talent. You can write and you can produce. You have everything you need. Just go back to Detroit and do it."

He did.

After he did, I wasn't the biggest Motown fan because I felt like the soul had become too soft, but I respected the hell out of Gordy's business acumen. He saw a market, and he captured it.

Stoller Some say Sam Cooke invented soul music in the fifties, and some say Ray Charles. Some say soul didn't come about

until later, in the sixties, with the advent of Otis Redding and Aretha Franklin. Others have told us that our productions for the Drifters began it all. Who can say?

The hits we made with that group surely had soul written all over them. But all that soul didn't just come from us. We wrote or cowrote or shaped some of their biggest hits—"On Broadway," "Dance with Me"—but, beginning with "There Goes My Baby," we served as the producers, directing the Drifters in the studio as they sang songs written by Doc Pomus and Morty Shuman ("This Magic Moment," "Save the Last Dance for Me"); Gerry Goffin and Carole King ("Some Kind of Wonderful," "Up on the Roof"); Burt Bacharach and Hal David ("Let the Music Play," "In the Land of

Make Believe"); and Barry Mann and Cynthia Weil, who collaborated with us on "On Broadway."

The Leiber-Stoller/Drifters collaboration had a five-year run. Yet during those years—1959 through 1963—the musical world took several turns. *Our* musical world took several turns. And those turns, both good and bad, mainly took place in the Brill Building. As our producer role became more pronounced, Jerry and I put more emphasis on our publishing company.

As Ray Charles once said, R&B is an adult music about adult matters. But this new music had a teeny-bop feel that younger writers like Ellie Greenwich and Jeff Barry could capture. It wasn't that Jerry and I couldn't turn out lighthearted material. The Coasters were nothing if *not* lighthearted. But the Coasters were framed in a dramatic context that wasn't specifically aimed at white teenage girls.

Black girl groups, like the Shirelles, were all the rage. Their "Will You Love Me Tomorrow?" another Goffin-King song, perfectly expressed the feminine mood of the day: that having sex with a guy would destroy his respect for her. Over in Detroit, Motown would soon get in the act with the Supremes, whose Holland-Dozier-Holland hits like "Baby Love" reflected teen longing and insecurities.

Meanwhile, our business was changing. We were signing writers to our publishing company. We were also working as producers. And in our production company, we mentored and supervised writer-producers, younger and more inexperienced versions of ourselves.

When we signed Jeff Barry, for instance, he had already had a hit, "Tell Laura I Love Her."

He walked into our office and said, "Ed Burton's publishing company has made me an offer. Will you match it?"

Jeff, who dressed like the Marlboro man, was very direct.

"We can't," I said. "We don't have that kind of money."

"Then how much will you offer?"

We offered him a much lower figure.

"I'll take it," he said.

"You will? How come?"

"Because I'll learn more here."

Leiber

Jeff learned a lot when he became one of our writers. But we also benefited greatly from his songwriting sense that was so in tune with teens. After we hired Jeff, we hired his girlfriend-writing partner who soon became his wife, Ellie Greenwich. The two of them were a terrific team. They wrote with an elegant simplicity and lack of self-consciousness. Ellie was a good singer who made demos of her songs that rivaled the released versions. We loved her talent as well as her extravagant beehive hairdo.

We also signed a friend of Jeff's named Neil Diamond. We knew he had talent, and he was happy to be on board, but we somehow assumed Jeff and Ellie would produce him. When they didn't, we figured that, for whatever reason, the chemistry wasn't right for Neil at our place. We gave him his release. Neil wound up with Bert Berns, who, together with Wexler, Ahmet, and Nesuhi, started a new label called Bang!

Stoller

At one point we formed a new publishing firm with Burt Bacharach and Hal David. Burt was the most perfectly casual dresser ever to stroll down Broadway. Even his hair was perfectly casual. Hal looked like an accountant. Together, of course, they made magic, especially the string of hits they wrote for Dionne Warwick, whom we had used for years as a background singer along with her sister, Dee Dee, and their aunt Cissy Houston.

The Brill Building was the Wild West of self-styled publishers and writers focusing on pop R&B. It was loose and fast and everyone wanted in on the act. While we focused on writing, producing, and publishing, we lacked the vision of an empire and the ambition of someone like Don Kirshner.

I met Donnie when he was delivering sheet music and song demos to Atlantic. He gave intensity new meaning. He introduced himself as a publisher before he owned a single copyright. He was both eager and deadly serious.

Leiber Nasty day in Manhattan. Wind howling. Below freezing. Cabs stalled in drifts of snow. Mike and I are slowly crossing Broadway. Nothing's moving except this guy coming toward us.

He stops us and greets us like he's a long-lost cousin. We don't recognize him.

"Donnie Kirshner," he says, sticking out his hand and shaking ours.

"You guys are the greatest," he continues. "I want to start a publishing company with you."

"Well, Donnie," I said, "we have our own little operation, plus we're working closely with Atlantic."

"You can get out of it," he said. "I'll help you. I'll make you a fortune."

"This isn't the best place for a meeting," I said. "It's four degrees out and I'm freezing my ass off."

"We'll be equal partners," said Donnie.

"We'll talk about it some other time," I said.

We never did.

Who knew that Donnie had the golden ear? Who knew that his

Aldon Music would wind up with a writing stable that included Carole King, Gerry Goffin, Neil Sedaka, Howard Greenfield, Barry Mann, and Cynthia Weil—to name a few? Who knew his publishing firm would ultimately be worth millions?

Stoller   And who knew that a simple statement on the part of an accountant would lead to a major crisis?

"I think you should audit Atlantic," said our accountant.

"Why?" both Jerry and I wanted to know.

"Standard business practice," he said. "And good business practice. Doing so doesn't say that you don't trust Atlantic. It merely says that you're being true to your corporate responsibilities."

Jerry looked at me. "What do you think, Mike?"

"Business is business," I said. "I'm sure Ahmet and Wexler will understand."

Jerry wasn't totally convinced. He was right.

Wexler went wild. "You've made thousands of dollars here!" he screamed. "Why in hell would you fuck up our relationship like this?"

"That's not our intention," I told Wexler. "We're just following our accountant's suggestions. Wow, I'm really surprised by your reaction."

"Do you work for that schmuck or does that schmuck work for you?"

"He gave us professional advice."

"Well, if you want my advice, call off the dogs—and do it now!"

By then it was too late; the wheels were already in motion. When the audit came back, it showed that Atlantic owed us $18,000.

"You got a choice," said Wexler. "I cut you a check for the eighteen thousand today and you'll never work with any of our artists again. Or you can forgo the money and it will be business as usual."

Jerry and I didn't hesitate. "Okay, we'll forget about the money."

"Good," said Wexler who then, despite his promise, kept us from producing any more Atlantic artists for quite a while.

"We're screwed," said Jerry.

Fortunately, we had found work at United Artists, where our attorney, Lee Eastman, negotiated an even more lucrative deal. Beyond signing and producing Jay and the Americans, we also had hits with Mike Clifford, a sort of white Johnny Mathis ("Close to Cathy" and "What to Do with Laurie"), and the Exciters ("Tell Him"). It was fun while it lasted, but it didn't last long because Art Talmadge, who hired us, lost out in a power play and, once again, we were without a record company home.

Strangely enough, we weren't worried. Our minds were too fixated on music to get uptight over business. The business was fueled by the music, and by this point we realized that music was something we could handle.

In the early sixties, Brazilian music was everywhere. Stan Getz and Charlie Byrd's version of "Desafinado" was being played on the radio and, in the back of my mind, I was toying with the idea of incorporating the samba.

One day, after the UA debacle, I remember fooling with a Latin motif. Playing always helped lighten my mood. When Jerry heard me, his mood lightened as well. He started writing, and then he started singing along.

A half hour later, we had the bare bones of a story.

> *I said, "Hey, little mama, let's sit down, have a drink*
> *And dig the band"*

She said, "Drink, you fink, oh, fiddle-de-dink, I can dance
With a drink in my hand"

When we got through, I asked Jerry, "Is it a hit?"

"Who cares?" he said. "I like it."

It wasn't really a bossa nova, but turned out to be the first single of our new record company.

At the end of 1962, seven years after we had folded Spark to go into business with Atlantic, we were out of business with Atlantic and UA and into a new venture.

Were we nuts to do it?

18

Tigers and Daisies

Leiber By nature, I look ahead, not back. But as we muddled our way through the Atlantic mess, it was tough not to remember what we had done. Ahmet and Wexler never tired of telling us how we had brought back the Drifters, and how the Drifters had taken Atlantic out of a slump that had begun when Ray Charles left their label in the late fifties. We'd done big production numbers that industry insiders were saying revolutionized the sound of pop. I wasn't thinking that way, and neither was Mike, but when other producers went to Manny's Music store on Forty-eighth Street and asked for the Leiber-Stoller kit, we realized we were forging some kind of new template.

Stoller I'll never forget this story:

A newly hired clerk was working at Manny's when a young producer made the request.

"Give me the Leiber-Stoller kit," he said.

"What's that?" asked the clerk.

"You know," said the producer, "all those crazy percussion instruments that Jerry Leiber and Mike Stoller use to produce their records."

"I'm not sure what you're looking for," said the clerk.

"Well then, this will help," said the producer as he pulled out "This Magic Moment," the Doc Pomus–Morty Shuman song we'd produced for the Drifters. "Identify the drums and then rent them to me."

Turned out, the clerk was a percussion man himself. "No problem," he said. "I've been working as a studio drummer for years."

The record played. The clerk listened attentively.

"Do you get it now?" asked the producer.

"What I get," said the clerk, "is that these guys used every drum in this store, plus a half dozen drums that don't even exist."

Leiber   The music business was always filled with hucksters. I didn't mind them. Some were my friends. Many of them were crazy, entertaining, wild, witty, brilliant. Some were stupid. The best had a canny ability to make the right connections. They were the guys who liked to say that they could sell ice cubes to Eskimos. And the truth was that they were, in fact, cold-blooded hustlers.

Mike and I lacked both that talent and inclination. And yet, knowing that we weren't fools, we figured that, given the entrepreneurial environment in which we had thrived, we could thrive even more by starting another label. A few years before, we had had a big hit with the Clovers. Mike had written one of his groovy R&B melodies. I wrote the words to go with it:

I took my troubles down to Madame Ruth
You know that gypsy with the gold-capped tooth

She's got a pad down at Thirty-fourth and Vine
Sellin' little bottles of
Love potion number nine

I told her that I was a flop with chicks
I've been this way since 1956
She looked at my palm and she made a magic sign
She said, "What you need is
Love potion number nine"

Stoller
We always loved the word *nine* because it resonates in song. Remember "Riot in Cell Block #9"? When my doctor holds a stethoscope to my back, he always asks me to say "nine."

Nine's a lucky number.

Leiber
In anticipation of the advent of esoteric stimulants in the sixties, some have seen "Love Potion No. 9" as a comedic forerunner of LSD or ganja. Bullshit. That stuff wasn't for me. Booze was always my thing. My most meaningful stimulant was cognac. I wrote by the glow of a burning Camel cigarette in one hand and a brandy snifter in the other. Smokes and Courvoisier were the dependable companions to my creative process. Although I am reluctantly and regretfully long reformed, no one has ever enjoyed—and thrived on—smoking and drinking more than I did. All this is to say that "Love Potion No. 9" does not represent a disguised advocacy for other kinds of drugs in the pre-hippie era.

Stoller

We started our own label called Tiger Records. This meant that we would not only produce, but we would press, and, through independents, distribute our own records. It also meant that we'd have to promote them—that is, advertise them and secure airplay. The promotion aspect of the business is where we'd have problems.

Nonetheless, we recruited the members of the "Love Potion No. 9" Clovers and their new lead singer, Roosevelt "Tippie" Hubbard, and had them do "Bossa Nova Baby." *Billboard* loved it, chose it as "Pick of the Week," but the public never heard it. We knew nothing about the crass commercial necessity of securing airplay. The single bombed, and so did our attempt to build up a label. Elvis rescued the tune later by recording it for *Fun in Acapulco* and pushing it into the Top Ten, but of course Elvis was on RCA, not Tiger. Given our uncertain finances, there wasn't much left in Tiger's tank, so we folded the label. But less than a year later, bruised but not defeated, we resuscitated Tiger and added a sister label, Daisy Records.

Our front-line team consisted of the songwriters Ellie Greenwich and Jeff Barry, who understood what was happening in teen pop—plus writer-arranger and all-around maestro Artie Butler, a wonderfully talented guy. It was Jeff who produced Cathy Saint singing "Big Bad World."

We were sure we had a hit. The DJ copies were sent out to the distributors and we waited for reactions. As it happened, I was on jury duty downtown, where we listened to a long, drawn-out argument from Monday through Thursday. Mercifully, on Friday morning the judge announced that the case had been settled and we were excused. I took the subway back to the Brill Building. As I walked through the door of our office, I heard a terrifying cry from somewhere on the floor. I ran out in the hallway. A woman was screaming, "The President! President Kennedy has been shot dead!"

Leiber

It takes no genius to understand that in light of the assassination of President John F. Kennedy, no radio station was going to broadcast anything other than news related to that terrible event.

Of much less significance was the fact that our new releases bit the dust. After those dark days in Dallas, there was neither love nor joy in anyone's heart. At the same time, though, songwriters go on writing, producers go on producing, and labels go on releasing records. We kept trudging.

We tried with an instrumental group who had a terrific guitarist named Roy Buchanan. Roy would find fame of his own, but the band, called the Temptations, would have problems. First problem came when we were told of another Temptations group, on Motown. Our Temptations' first single, "Trophy Run," was already released—so we had to call it back and reissue it under the name Bob Moore and the Temps. Meanwhile, the Motown Temps soon attained jukebox immortality and ours did not.

Stoller

Nineteen-sixty-four did not pass quickly. Our new labels were floundering, and there wasn't much life left in my marriage, either. Meryl and I had three young children whom we adored—Adam was two, Peter was four, and Amy was six. I wanted to give them a secure and happy home; I wanted the kind of calm domestic environment that I had never known. But my marriage to Meryl was anything but calm, secure, or happy. Our interests and temperaments were running in radically different directions. We both loved our children very much but disagreed about how to love them and how to educate them.

From left, Peter, Amy and Adam Stoller,
Christmas, New York, 1963.

I don't think either of us had the marriage we had envisioned when we walked down the aisle. Meryl would have preferred the security and stability of a husband who brought home a regular weekly salary with no surprises. She hoped that as a couple we would struggle to make ends meet as we tried to make the world a better place. I wanted to make the world a better place, too, but forget the weekly salary—and I sure as hell didn't want to have to struggle. When we moved from LA, it was actually quite a sacrifice for Meryl, who had adamantly not wanted to return to New York. But she generously and graciously did it because I wanted to.

I went into analysis and stayed there for much of the sixties. I reasoned that I could save this marriage if I better understood myself. But that reasoning, while it kept me from leaving for a couple of years, ultimately failed. I was unhappy. Work became everything. Work kept me out of the house, or behind closed doors in my workroom at home. In our Brill Building office, I could chain-smoke all day long, looking for the "lost chord." I could—at least for a while—forget the fact that my marriage was slowly falling apart.

Leiber Gaby and I had two great sons—Jed was born in 1959 and Oliver in 1961—but I would hardly call myself domesticated. If anything, due to Gaby's high-culture influence, I was more

From left, Jed and Oliver Leiber, 1965, East Hampton, New York.

sophisticated. I moved into Gaby's world, rather than vice versa. It was through Gaby that I met poets and painters who opened my eyes and mind to a modernity I had not before known. It isn't that I abandoned my culture. The cornball radio shows of the forties and the rocking blues rhythms of the fifties would inform every decade of my life. But, unlike Mike, who was always into serious music, I came by the serious stuff late in life. And it took a woman to guide me.

The path was never straight-ahead. One night I would be watching an Ionesco play off-Broadway. Another night I would be at the New School to hear Clement Greenberg discuss Jackson Pollock or at the 92nd Street Y, where Allen Ginsberg would be reading his poetry.

Our record label sure as hell wasn't prospering, but we were either too stupid or stubborn to give up. Then something happened that lifted our spirits past the point of no return. In the midst of the girl-group craze, we reconnected to our blues roots.

And suddenly, despite our business problems, the sun was shining.

Stoller

Stoller One day Joe Jones—not the Basie drummer, but a musician, entrepreneur/hustler, and performer who had hit with "You Talk Too Much"—walked into our office. Coming out of New Orleans, he embodied that city's unique brand of musical genius. Joe brought with him a group of artists: Moody and the Deltas, Alvin Robinson, and three girls he called the Meltones. We cut a deal with Joe, and Moody and the Deltas recorded one of Ellie and Jeff's songs, "Everybody Come Clap Your Hands," while Alvin cut "Something You Got."

Leiber We didn't write it; Chris Kenner, who recorded it first, did. We didn't arrange it—Joe Jones did. But we did produce it. And pound for pound, I'd call "Something You Got," as sung by Alvin Robinson, one of the grittiest performances of any era. I'd put Alvin up against Ray Charles, James Brown—you name 'em.

Alvin sang the thing like his life depended upon it. It didn't chart big, but it charted all the same.

Maybe the proudest we were of any of the Tiger releases was Bessie Banks's "Go Now." We didn't write that one either, but we produced it, and some people, me included, think it's the most overlooked soul performance of the sixties. Bessie's version did okay, but a year later—1965—it would become the Moody Blues' first Top Ten smash. Others cut it as well: Paul McCartney and Wings, Billy Preston, Cher. It would be a stretch to call "Go Now" a standard, but for my money, it's among our strongest productions, and Bessie's interpretation is by far the best.

Stoller Despite all this great stuff, we were hurting. We were hemorrhaging cash. We had families, small children, and big expenses. In the bitter cold music business, you're only as good as your last success. By that measure, we weren't very good. It looked like our second attempt to become label owners was destined to end the same way as our first—in flat-out failure. There seemed no way out of our financial hole until, one day after work, Jerry did what he most loved to do: hang out at Al and Dick's.

Al and Dick's

Leiber It was five o'clock when Mike came in and said, "Jer, we got less than $20,000 in the bank. At this rate, we'll be broke in no time. We gotta shut down our labels."

With that in mind, I was more eager than ever to forget my troubles. The idea of folding was depressing me, so I headed over to Al and Dick's, a local steak joint that catered to the music crowd. The place was packed. These were the blessed days when you could smoke wherever you wanted. I couldn't get close to the bar—they were four rows deep—so I found a table with a couple of the Brill Building hustlers, Goldie Goldmark and Juggy Gayles. Goldie was wearing a suit that looked like plastic. You could see your face in his jacket. Juggy was drinking screwdrivers.

"Juggy," said Goldie, "I heard about this place upstate. It's a building in a college. And inside this building they have this thing. It's called a think tank."

"You don't say," said Juggy.

"I do say," said Goldie. "And do you know what they do in the think tank?"

"I'm a record hawker," said Juggy. "How the fuck would I know what they do in a think tank?"

"Putz," said Goldie, tapping his finger on his forehead, "they think."

"Oh," said Juggy.

Such was the enlightened conversation at Al and Dick's.

Suddenly someone waved me over to his table. It was Hy Weiss, the proud owner of Big Town Records, a semi–big shot in the small-label music business. Hy, who looked like he worked in cement, was smoking a fat Monte Cristo. He was sitting with a man who was meticulously groomed. His pinstripe suit was black silk. Diamonds flashed from his gold cufflinks. A diamond flashed from the stick pin in his black Sulka tie.

"Jerry Leiber," said Hy, "meet the famous George Goldner."

Then Hy paused and added, "George, meet the famous Jerry Leiber."

"Of Leiber and Stoller?" asked Goldner.

"The same," I said.

"You're a pretty good little writer," said Goldner.

"I love your records," I told Goldner.

Goldner was practically singlehandedly responsible for some of the greatest hits of the day. His labels were legendary—Tico, Gone, End, Gee, Roulette, Rama. The word was that Goldner was hooked on the horses. In spite of his success on the charts, he'd find himself so deeply in debt that his "friend," Morris (Moishe) Levy, bailed him out by buying his labels for a song. Goldner had lost them all at the track.

Showing the man no respect, Hy said, "George is broke, Jerry, and he's begging me for a job. Would you pay this schmuck $350 a week to *hondl* records for you?"

With that, Hy blew a thick ring of smoke directly in Goldner's face.

Somehow Goldner maintained his dignity and quietly insisted that he was worth at least $500 a week. Hy kept insulting Goldner. Finally, Hy got up. "Gotta drain the monkey," he said, leaving George and me alone at the table.

Maybe it was the Maker's Mark I was drinking, but a lightbulb lit up my brain. "I'm going to be straight with you, George," I said. "Mike and I are about to go under. We need help. You got great ears and you know how to sell. I don't give a shit what Hy Weiss says. You've got the best track record of anyone on both coasts."

"Do you have unreleased product?" George asked.

"Yeah," I said.

"Is it any good?"

"To tell you the truth, George, I no longer know. We need fresh ears."

"I'll listen to what you got."

"When?"

"Now."

"Now?"

At that moment Hy returned to the table. George informed him that he was now a partner with Leiber and Stoller. Hy stared at me, incensed that I had screwed up his negotiations with Goldner. Meanwhile, George opened his silver case, took out a cigarette, lit it, and blew a stream of smoke into Hy's face, saying, "Now we'll see who the schmuck is."

And with that, our new partner went out into the night and up to our offices in the Brill Building.

Stoller

Jerry put it best: George Goldner had the musical taste of a fourteen-year-old girl. That, of course, is the highest compliment you can pay someone in the business of selecting and selling singles.

When I arrived at our office in the morning and saw Goldner sitting there, I was astonished but respectful. After all, George Goldner was the Mambo King. He had an amazing track record—no pun intended. He had signed Tito Puente, Tito Rodriguez, Joe Cuba, and Eddie Palmieri. He had put out Frankie Lymon and the Teenagers' "Why Do Fools Fall in Love," Little Anthony and the Imperials' "Tears on My Pillow" and "Shimmy, Shimmy, Ko-ko Bop," the Chantels' "Maybe" and the Flamingos' "I Only Have Eyes for You."

"How did you get in?" I asked him.

"Jerry gave me the keys and told me to listen to your stuff," said George. "I've been here all night listening to your acetates."

I was surprised. The man was impeccably dressed and looked fresh as a daisy. The pile of acetates he'd been reviewing had accumulated after our deal with United Artists had collapsed. Until then, UA had been reimbursing us for the cost of production. But when our exec at UA was canned, the arrangement was scrapped, and we were left with a bunch of songs and no way to release them.

Leiber When I walked in, Goldner was talking to Mike. George immediately turned to me and said, "This is it." And with that, he handed me an acetate without a label.

"Which song is it?" I asked.

"Put it on and play it," Goldner replied.

I did.

Oh God, I thought, *it's that piece of shit.*

"'Chapel of Love,'" George declared. "I'll bet my life on it."

I wanted to say, *You don't value your life very much*, but didn't. Guys like Goldner possessed special genius for divining hits.

Stoller

I liked "Chapel" the minute Jeff and Ellie sang it to me. They had composed it along with Phil Spector. Phil had recorded it with one of his groups.

I never heard that record, but apparently neither Jeff, Ellie, nor Phil liked the way it turned out. Jeff and Ellie wanted to recut it. They taught the song to the Meltones and asked Joe Jones to write the arrangement. On a weekend morning, they invited me to their apartment to help them put it together. I came up with an idea, an instrumental fill between the verses. I wrote out the parts for the horn section that would augment Joe's chart. A couple of days later, we all met up at Mira Sound. Joe's arrangement, which was probably ghosted by Wardell Quezergue, was extremely groovy and my additional horn lines worked like a charm. Then, as an afterthought, I improvised and overdubbed a line on celeste. As luck would have it, there was a set of orchestra bells in the studio that arranger-composer Artie Butler, who popped up at exactly the right moment, graciously agreed to play. I loved the record.

Leiber

I hated the record. I thought "Chapel of Love" was insipid, a trifling based on nothing but clichés. I wasn't even in the studio when Mike produced it. I couldn't stand listening to it.

On the other hand, I was the guy who recruited the great George Goldner to go through our inventory and see if he smelled any hits.

Without even a hint of hesitation, this was the record he selected. I'd be a fool to overrule the man who, when it came to marketing, I'd chosen to overrule us. Besides; Mike, no fool himself, liked the goddamn thing.

Stoller
The Meltones were two sisters, Barbara Ann and Rosa Lee Hawkins, and their cousin Joan Marie Johnson. We had to change their name because Mel Torme called his group the Mel-Tones. There was talk of naming them Little Miss and the Muffets. I suggested the Dixie Cups.

They were wonderful in the studio, where Ellie, a great harmonizer, taught them their parts. Jeff was expert at setting the groove. All the elements fell into place.

Jerry thought my version was better than Phil's, but he still didn't like the song. At that point, I didn't have the energy to argue with him. And now, months later, the surprise came when Jerry didn't have the energy to argue with Goldner.

Leiber
"Chapel of Love" hit the top of the pop charts in the spring of 1964 and stayed there for three weeks.

It was the first US-made record to hit #1 since the British Invasion.

In the Golden Age of the Girl Group, we finally had a bestselling group of our own. The Marvelettes were marvelous, the Supremes supreme, and the Ronettes resplendent. But the Dixie Cups, three humble gals from Louisiana, were giving them all a run for their money.

We wanted a label that would work.

So we rejoiced when money started coming in. At last a Leiber and Stoller label looked like it might actually make some noise in an industry that seemed to have been taken over by four kids from Liverpool.

20

The Bird Flies

Stoller   When the Beatles hit in early 1964, I immediately liked them; I felt their enormous charm.

I later learned that the demo they had submitted to British Decca contained two of our songs, "Searchin'" and "Three Cool Cats." They later recorded "Kansas City." Paul also did a number of versions of "Kansas City," John did "Stand by Me" and "Hound Dog," and Ringo recorded "I Keep Forgettin'."

Leiber   I didn't care that they knew our stuff. I wasn't crazy about the early Beatles because they were not funky enough.

We didn't experience the British Invasion as a threat. We were delighted that many of the English groups covered our songs.

Stoller "Chapel of Love" was issued as our first release on Red Bird, the name of our new label. With that one song, we were off and running.

George had picked a winner. He had also understood that, given our financial weakness, we couldn't give him a salary. We did, however, give him one-third ownership of the label. When it came to sales and promotion, Jerry and I didn't know diddly, while George was a proven master.

The team was in place: Jerry, Goldner, and I were the owners. But Ellie Greenwich and Jeff Barry were the primary songwriters and also did production of their own. Artie Butler was chief arranger; Brooks Arthur at Mira Sound was our engineer. Then along came George Morton.

Leiber I called him Shadow, and, just like that, he became Shadow Morton, a guy who appeared in the room without your realizing that he ever walked in. And he was never there when you looked for him. Shadow was elusive. He was good looking and packed a self-invented mythology that intrigued me. For a guy from New York, he spoke with a strange Southern drawl. He had a sweet temperament and was physically strong as a bull. Mostly, he had a genius for writing songs that were teenage soap operas. I loved Shadow and everything he did for Red Bird.

Stoller Shadow found the Shangri-Las, who, along with the Dixie Cups, became the engine of what would soon be Red Bird's hit-making machine. What Leiber and Stoller were to the Coasters and Jeff and Ellie were to the Dixie Cups, Shadow Morton was to the Shangri-Las.

The group consisted of four girls—twins Mary Ann and Marge Ganser and two sisters who looked like twins, Mary and Betty Weiss. The Weiss girls were blondes, the Gansers brunettes. They dressed in leather boots over tight jeans. The Shangri-Las were the perfect white "bad girls" of the day.

An old copy of *Billboard* from 1964 describes their first Red Bird single, "Remember (Walkin' in the Sand)," this way: "For those who like a different sound, try this haunting delivery." And deliver it did. It sold a million copies.

Leiber As a producer, Shadow threw in everything but the kitchen sink. He created a cacophony, but one that made musical sense—and story sense to boot. The follow-up to "Remember (Walkin' in the Sand)" was an even more spectacular success. "Leader of the Pack" reached #1 for the Shangri-Las. It was teen melodrama, and teens went nuts for it.

In the studio, I helped Shadow with the special effects of roaring motorcycles and screaming seagulls. A few months later, he wrote another sappy mini-saga for the Shangri-Las, "I Can Never Go Home Anymore." I was sure this one was just too cornball to hit. I was wrong. It soared to #6 in 1965.

Even though Mike and I stood on the sidelines as supervisors for many Red Bird hits, we produced a couple of smashes of our own. John Taylor came up with "The Boy from New York City" for his group, the Ad Libs. We related to the hip lyrics—"he's really down, and he's no clown / he's cute in his mohair suit / he's the most, from coast to coast." We took the Ad Libs into the studio where Artie Butler's funky chart kicked the single into orbit. It was our biggest hit on Blue Cat, the subsidiary label we looked on as more R&B than pop.

Stoller

One day Jeff and Ellie brought the Dixie Cups to Mira Sound for a touchup for the vocals of "People Say," a tune we'd recorded a few days earlier. While we were mixing in the booth, engineer Brooks Arthur, simply by chance, opened the mics. In the studio, the Dixie Cups were creating a sound, just for fun, that knocked us out. It turned out to be an old Mardi Gras song called "Iko Iko." We decided to cut it then and there. No band was present. But that didn't matter. We'd go minimal and become the band ourselves. Jeff and Ellie picked up a Coke bottle, a plastic bowl, and a few can openers. That became the percussion. There was also a souvenir kalimba box from the West Indies, a sort of giant version of an African thumb piano. I found a way to tune it and used it to play a bass line. The Dixie Cups sang the song with tremendous feeling and authenticity. When we were finished, we loved it. And when "Iko Iko" was released, the public loved it, too. We had another Top Twenty hit.

21

The Magnificent Merger That Never Happened

Leiber In 1965, Jerry Wexler called me out of the blue. We hadn't heard a peep from him for quite a while. But now the tables were turned. Red Bird was red hot and Atlantic was ice cold.

Although the accounting debacle with Atlantic had left a sour taste in our mouths, we still had warm feelings for Ahmet, Wexler, and Nesuhi. Let bygones be bygones.

"I have an idea," Wexler said. "What would you think about merging Red Bird and Atlantic? You have creative talents we lack, and we have a sales/distribution system second to none. Let's get together and talk."

"I'd have to bring in Mike and Goldner."

"Of course," said Wexler, "and I'd have to bring in Ahmet and Nesuhi. But at least it's worth a preliminary discussion."

"I'd want to bring our lawyer as well," I said.

"The more the merrier," said Wexler. "We'll put all our ideas on the table and see what happens."

Stoller

The idea was exciting for more than one reason: George Goldner, despite his extraordinary ability to pick and push hits, was someone we could never trust. Some employees claimed he was selling our records out of the back of the warehouse and pocketing the cash. There were rumors that he was back at the track, where his losses were piling up. A merger with Atlantic would mean close supervision over George's practices, something that Jerry and I, who stayed busy in the studio, weren't able to handle. If Goldner was stealing, as we strongly suspected, Wexler would quickly catch him. Also the thought of being partners with people I thought of as kindred spirits sounded wonderful.

I readily agreed to the meeting.

Leiber

The Oak Room at the Plaza Hotel was a stuffy restaurant where blue-haired old ladies gossiped over tea. It seemed a strange choice for this summit, but, then again, this summit turned out to be the strangest meeting of our strange career.

Wexler, Ahmet, and Nesuhi were there representing Atlantic. Mike and I, plus Goldner and our attorney, Lee Eastman, represented Red Bird.

"Drinks?" Ahmet offered.

"You're goddamn right," said Goldner.

Goldner hit the booze hard. Before the salads arrived, he had put away two martinis and was working on a third.

Wexler began the discussion with the big picture: they had what we needed and we had what they wanted.

"Who needs a label that's going down the toilet?" asked Goldner, referring to Atlantic.

"We're hardly going down the toilet," said Ahmet.

"With the shit you're putting out, it won't be long."

Ahmet was shocked. So were we. Goldner could be crude at times, but this was hardly the time or place.

Stoller

We apologized for Goldner's behavior and tried to keep him quiet. We canceled his order for a fourth martini.

Then Lee Eastman started to expound. At least our attorney would speak in the voice of reason.

"It's absolutely unreasonable to see how this merger could benefit anyone but Atlantic," he said.

"But you haven't heard the terms," Wexler argued.

"The terms are beside the point," said Lee. "You have little to offer us, and we have everything to offer you."

"Wait till you hear the offer," said Wexler.

"I didn't know we were prepared to make a formal offer," said Ahmet, sounding confused.

George piped in. "Him and Wexler are supposed to be running Atlantic, but the right hand doesn't know what the left hand is doing. Looks to me like they're just jerking each other off. Aside from a free lunch, this is a goddamn waste of time."

"I'd have to agree," said Lee.

I looked at Jerry and Jerry looked at me.

Neither one of us knew what was happening. But by then it didn't matter. Ahmet and Nesuhi had left.

Leiber

Back at the office, it didn't take Mike and me long to figure it out. Goldner wanted to sabotage the deal because the deal would make him accountable. He'd be caught stealing. Lee Eastman wanted to sabotage the deal because he was getting not only 5 percent of our writing and production income, but also plenty of legal fees from Red Bird. If a merger went through, he feared we would be using Atlantic's lawyers instead of him. But reasons and motives didn't matter. The enterprise was beyond repair. The deal was screwed.

Stoller It got worse. Ahmet's reading of the meeting was: *Wexler and Leiber and Stoller are trying to buy me out.* I don't know how he got that idea, but for the longest time Ahmet treated us like pariahs. And it seemed that Ahmet no longer trusted Wexler. The chill between Ahmet and Wexler went on for years.

That meeting was a fiasco, and the worst part was that, for the time being, Goldner was still in the driver's seat.

Leiber A couple of months passed.

I was walking down Broadway, not far from our offices in the Brill Building. I had just bought two pairs of red suspenders from a street vendor for my little boys when an enormous black hand draped itself over my right shoulder. "Sal wants to see you." (Sal isn't his real name.)

"Who's Sal?" I asked.

"A guy you need to meet."

"Why?" I asked.

"He's a big fan of yours."

With that, the dude firmly led me around the corner, where we walked into a little deli I'd never noticed before.

Sal looked like a guy you'd see sitting in the first row at Madison Square Garden. He wasn't pretty, and his cigar didn't smell sweet. He introduced his guys, Tutti and John. They were big boys.

"Do you like steak, Jerry?" asked Sal.

"I like steak," I said.

"They'll make you a steak. They'll make you a beautiful porter-house. Let me order you a steak."

"A steak's a little heavy, Sal. I'll have a bagel and cream cheese."

"A bagel with extra cream cheese!" Sal yelled to the waiter. "And coffee. Jerry, would you like a nice hot cup of coffee?"

"Coffee would be great."

"Cream and sugar?"

"Cream and sugar, yes."

The bagel arrived with enough cream cheese to satisfy half of Philadelphia. The coffee was light and sweet.

"Is the coffee alright, Jerry?" asked Sal.

"The coffee's fine."

"What you got in the bag?" Sal wanted to know.

"Suspenders."

"You wear suspenders?"

"They're for my kids."

"How many kids you got, Jerry?"

"Two."

"Boys or girls?"

"Two boys."

"That's nice. I love kids. It's good to know you have kids."

A wave of fear passed over me. Then I remembered that the boys were out in East Hampton with Gaby—and I was glad.

"Are you wondering why I called this meeting?" Sal asked.

"I'm curious, sure."

"Because I wanted to meet my partner face to face."

"Partner? In what venture?"

"Aren't you in the record business, Jerry?"

"Of course."

"Well, I am, too. What do we call it? Red Bird Records. And Blue Bird. That's another one of our labels, isn't it?"

"No, it's Blue Cat."

"Blue Cat, Blue Bird, it's all green. It's all money."

"I'm confused, Sal."

"Nothing to be confused about, Jerry. I'll lay it out for you. Goldner is my partner. You're Goldner's partner. So that makes us all partners. Simple, ain't it?"

"I thought Mike and I were Goldner's *only* partners."

"You thought wrong. Goldner brought us into the business when he needed some funding. He didn't tell you that?"

"I'm afraid not."

"I'm gonna level with you, Jerry. You're in a bind and you need help. So think of it like this: What does a Catholic boy do when he's in trouble? He goes to his priest. And what does a Jewboy do when he's in trouble?"

"He calls his lawyer?" I asked.

Sal laughed but then got serious. "You're funny, Jerry, but you're wrong. A Jewboy in trouble goes to see his rabbi. You're a Jewboy in trouble, and I'm your rabbi."

I didn't argue.

I went back to the office and told Mike.

"Shit," Mike said. "What do we do now?"

"Nothing," I said. "Maybe it'll go away."

But of course it didn't go away. Guys started showing up in our office, brutes who could barely fit through the door.

"We gotta use your conference room," they said.

Once again, I didn't argue.

Stoller I approached Goldner.

"George," I said, "how in the world could you do this to us?"

"Do what?" George asked.

"Put us in jeopardy by bringing in the wiseguys."

"It's only temporary," George said. "Once I pay them off, they'll be out of here. It's nothing to worry about."

It was everything to worry about.

Jerry and I, two nice Jewish boys, were somehow in business with the wiseguys.

Leiber I sought the advice of my father-in-law, Saemy Rosenberg.

"I'm having lunch today with my friend Guy de Rothschild," he said. "Please join us."

"What I have to ask you is very personal," I said.

"Guy is my closest friend, Jerry. He knows absolutely everything about my family. I trust him with my life."

I met them at Luchow's, a venerable old German restaurant on Fourteenth Street. Saemy and his friend Baron Guy de Rothschild were seated at a quiet corner table. They were dressed like English gentlemen and spoke in distinguished European accents.

Saemy introduced me to Rothschild in glowing terms. "There is no finer songwriter in the country today," he said. "He and his partner have enjoyed unprecedented success."

"Until now," I hastened to add.

Then I told them the story of George Goldner, Sal, and Sal's friends. They listened attentively. When I was through, they spoke between themselves in German. I knew some Yiddish, but I couldn't quite understand their comments.

Finally Saemy spoke in English. "Guy and I agree, Jerry, that you have but one course of action."

"What's that?" I asked.

"Well," Saemy Rosenberg continued, "what do they want from you? Money? Jerry, anything you can buy for money is cheap."

Stoller I couldn't have agreed more. Seeing these thugs hanging around our office, acting as though they were part of the enterprise, was a weight that neither of us could bear. There was only one answer.

22

The Bird Dies

Stoller   It was a Monday in March of 1966.

Monday seemed like the best day to do it. Jerry and I had talked about it all weekend and we didn't see any other way out. On one hand, it seemed ridiculous. Financially, it was absolutely crazy. But there are times when money can't dictate terms. This was one of those times.

George was in his office when Jerry and I walked in. He was reading the *Daily Racing Form*. As always, he was dressed like a bank president. His sapphire pinkie ring matched his cufflinks.

Leiber   "George," I said, "we have a big surprise for you. A beautiful gift."

"What did I do to deserve a gift?" he asked, smiling sweetly.

"Everything," I said.

"What's the gift?"

"Red Bird Records," I said.

"Red Bird Records?" he asked. "I don't get it."

"You do get it. We're giving it to you."

"Giving me what?"

"The business. Red Bird Records. It's yours."

"You're crazy. It's worth a fortune. I don't have a fortune."

"You don't need a fortune," I said. "You don't need a thing. We're giving you our share of the label."

"Why?"

"We're tired of the record business. We want to concentrate on writing and publishing. Who's more deserving than you?"

George was genuinely moved—so moved, in fact, tears welled up in his eyes.

"I don't know what to say," he said.

"I do," I replied. "To make it official, Mike and I are selling you our two-thirds ownership of Red Bird Records for a dollar. Give us a dollar and the deal is done."

George took out his billfold and saw that it was empty. "Gee, fellas," he said. "When I left for work today my wife must have taken out my money. She was afraid I'd go to the track."

"No problem," said Mike, pulling out a dollar and handing it to me. "Jerome, lend this dollar to Mr. Goldner."

"Mr. Goldner," I said, handing the buck to George, "we are lending you a dollar."

"Mike and Jerry," said Goldner, handing the buck back to Mike, "here's a dollar for your label. But put in the contract that you won't press me for the return of the loan."

Mike took the dollar and shook George's hand.

"I don't fuckin' believe this," said George.

"Believe it," I said. "This deal is done. We're gone."

The next day we built a brick wall separating our office space from George's.

On his side of the wall, George attempted to keep Red Bird going. Within a few months, however, he sold all the master recordings to record company owner Shelby Singleton in Nashville.

Stoller
We started our string of little labels at the end of 1962. By spring of 1966, we were out. It had been a helluva run. Looking back, we were amazed at the number of hits. The last one to chart, ironically enough, was called "Past, Present and Future," sung by the Shangri-Las. History would establish Red Bird as one of the most successful independent labels of the era.

Our material rivaled the best of Motown. But the great bulk of our material was generated by others—primarily Ellie, Jeff, and Shadow. True, our supervision was critical. We helped sculpt the songs and oversaw many productions. But the girl group aesthetic was not our aesthetic. We appreciated it; we encouraged it; we profited from it; but we did not love it the way we loved the blues we had written for Big Mama Thornton or the rollicking R&B we had written and produced for the Coasters.

Before we gave Red Bird to Goldner, we had toyed with other signings. In that regard, you might say we made mistakes. We had a chance to sign sensational acts—Sam and Dave, the Young Rascals, and Steely Dan. We heard their talent. We knew they were great, but we thought if we had more hits, we might be stuck doing this for the rest of our lives. Our hearts weren't into being label bosses anymore. We were thirty-three. We were spent, and our interests were moving into areas beyond youth culture, even as that culture was growing bigger.

For better or worse, we had to go a different way.

23

Happenings

Stoller Among the arty avant-garde crowd in the New York City of the late sixties, happenings were all the rage. You'd get a call from a friend that four painters, a trapeze artist, and three bongo players had rented a loft and were putting on a performance in which you were invited to participate. You could show up with your tuba, your crayons, or your tap shoes and do whatever you liked. The Age of Aquarius was upon us.

I was invited to one such happening in 1966. It had been a rough year. After great agonizing, I had moved out of the house and into the Croyden Hotel on the Upper East Side. My marriage was beyond repair. I spent the weekends with the kids, took them on vacations, and spent as much time with them as possible. But of course it wasn't the same. Our family had fallen apart, and the result was an oppressive sadness that I felt every day. I began dating other women, but with extreme care. I did not want to get overly involved. Happenings, therefore, had a certain appeal to me. My friend Hilly Elkins was in the thick of the action. He produced *Oh!*

Calcutta! the trendy play that gave Broadway its first taste of full-frontal nudity.

"Hey, Mike," he said one night over the phone, "show up at the Armory on Twenty-sixth Street around nine; there's going to be a happening."

I showed up with Penelope, a Greek gal I was dating at the time. The happening revolved around a tennis game between painter Robert Rauschenberg and composer John Cage over an electronically wired net. When the ball hit the net all sorts of lights went off. The evening alternated between vaguely interesting and vaguely boring. Afterwards, Hilly invited us all over to Sardi's, where Jerry popped in for the post-happening festivities.

I was seated next to Sheila Sullivan, Hilly's girlfriend, who mentioned her roommate, Corky Hale.

"I know her work," I said. "She's a great harpist."

"She's a piano player," said Sheila.

"A harpist," I insisted. "One of my favorite records is a ten-inch LP Corky Hale made with the singer Kitty White on Pacific Jazz. Corky's a fabulous harpist."

"Pianist." Sheila was unrelenting.

Overhearing our conversation, Jerry said, "I met her once in LA. Tell her to drop by our office. We can use her on some demos."

Turned out that I was right, and so was Sheila; Corky's a great harpist *and* pianist. And, to me, she became a great deal more.

Leiber
I got a call from Tennessee Williams. He suggested we meet to discuss turning his 1953 play *Camino Real* into a musical.

I was to arrive at the Elysée, a swanky little hotel on the East Side a week from Saturday at eight. "Sit at the bar," said Tennessee,

Corky Hale, 1955.

"order a martini and, after you finish your first drink, have the bartender call me."

I did precisely as I was told. I was more into bourbon than gin and vermouth, but out of respect for Mr. Williams's literary genius, I followed the instructions to the letter. After my first martini, the bartender called the playwright to tell him I was waiting. Fifteen minutes passed and I was hungry. I gulped down a large quantity of peanuts. And just as the great man himself arrived, looking especially suave in a gray cashmere topcoat and black fedora, I grabbed another handful of peanuts.

"We're going to a party," Tennessee told me. "Let us leave immediately."

As we walked through the bar to the lobby of the hotel, I didn't know what to do with the peanuts. So when the doorman opened the door for us and signaled the waiting limo, I handed him the peanuts. Tennessee witnessed it all.

"My dear Mr. Leiber," he said, "it is terribly gauche to tip a doorman in peanuts. I do believe they prefer cash."

The party was at a brownstone in the West Village. The minute Tennessee walked through the door, he was greeted as a conquering hero. The adoring crowd was overwhelmingly gay. I happened to spot a young ingénue I knew from Elaine's, my favorite evening hangout in the city. As Tennessee disappeared into the next room to mingle among his admirers, I chatted up the young actress. I had several more drinks and, because I still hadn't eaten, the alcohol had me more assertive than usual. I guess I was coming on strong—not that the lady seemed to mind—when I felt a man's arms encircle me from behind.

"I see you're having a good time," said Tennessee.

"I am," I said.

"Well, I'm afraid it's time to leave."

Tennessee walked me out the door and halfway down the front steps before he turned around to rejoin the party, making it clear that *I* was leaving, not him. I presumed my behavior had embarrassed him. First, the peanuts; now, the girl.

"What about *Camino Real?*" I asked. "Weren't we going to discuss it?"

"We were," said Tennessee Williams, "but we aren't."

And we never did.

Stoller

I felt an instant attraction and rapport with Corky. In truth, I had fallen madly in love with her in 1955 while I was listening to that ten-inch LP. Kitty White sang exquisitely, and the harp was one of the most beautiful things I had ever heard. It was just harp and voice, nothing else. On the back of the album was a photo of the adorable harpist. I was smitten.

Then, eleven years later, on a crisp fall afternoon in October 1966, she walked into our office and my life has never been the same.

At the time, I was committed to noncommitment. The pain of my failed marriage was still acute. Marriage was out, but dating was in. In fact, when I met Corky I was kinda going steady with several different women.

Mike and Corky on an early date, New York, 1967.

But it was different with Corky. We had a million things in common. Jazz was at the top of the list. Corky was not only beautiful, but a jazz player of the first rank. As music lovers, we were perfectly compatible. Our first date, in fact, was to see jazz guitarist Joe Beck. Earlier in the evening, over dinner at Benihana, I was fascinated as Corky told me a little about herself.

She was a Jewish girl from a small farm town in the Midwest. Although she had accompanied Tony Bennett and had once been Billie Holiday's pianist—Billie adored Corky and called her "my little girl"—she had none of the pretensions of a hip jazz chick. She was down to earth, funny, and smart. She didn't get high, she didn't try to impress me with her accomplishments, and she didn't seem overly impressed with mine. In fact, she hadn't even heard of Leiber and Stoller.

Her musical experience was vast. One of the gigs she enjoyed most, she told me, was with Liberace in Vegas. "He's a fabulous entertainer," Corky said, "and I loved working with him."

Notwithstanding Liberace's flamboyance, though, Corky's favorite pianist was Bill Evans. On many occasions, Corky and I caught Evans at the Village Vanguard, where we were spellbound by Bill's harmonic inventions.

Corky told me about her time at the University of Wisconsin where she joined the NAACP and was so moved by the work of Martin Luther King, Jr., that she wrote up her will and left him her entire inheritance. A committed liberal, she discussed with me the problems that she was having with a famous male singer. This singer, for whom she was playing the piano, was starting to get on her nerves.

A week or so later she left with this guy and his orchestra for some out-of-town gigs. They weren't due back for three or four weeks. Four days later, though, Corky called to say she was back in New York.

"What happened?" I asked.

"I told him to take his job and shove it."

"How come?"

"First of all, he was talking to the audience when he pointed to a Puerto Rican busboy and said, 'Here's that spic again.' I could have killed him then. And if that weren't enough, after the show he went on a tirade against interracial dating, calling miscegenation a crime against nature. I couldn't take it anymore. I told him I couldn't work with anyone who talked and thought the way he did."

That's Corky.

Leiber There were happenings in the art galleries and lofts all around the city, but, every night, there was also something of a happening at Elaine's, the restaurant on Second Avenue at Eighty-eighth Street that became a watering hole for a pride of literary lions.

Stoller I was also a regular at Elaine's. In fact, when I moved to the Croyden Hotel, only a few blocks away from the restaurant, Elaine's became my living room. I was there every night, drinking, eating and playing after-hours poker with Jack Richardson, Jack Gelber, Arthur Kopit, and "Coco" Brown. Sometimes the game drifted over to the Park Avenue apartment of Woody Allen and his wife, Louise Lasser. One sensed an air of impermanence in their relationship. I say that because the interior décor consisted of one poker table and eight folding chairs. The deli spread was laid out on the radiator cover.

Woody was another denizen of Elaine's. Elaine Kaufman was a character, a watchful ever-present den mother for writers and show-biz types who liked to cavort and bullshit late into the night.

Leiber

Norman Mailer was the big star at Elaine's. Along with Bruce Jay Friedman, Gay Talese, Terry Southern, Kurt Vonnegut, Frank Conroy, Pete Hamill, Bill Styron and a host of others, Mailer would show up on a weekly basis. Paul Desmond, the alto saxist who had been the soul of Dave Brubeck's popular jazz group in the fifties, was among the wittiest. We all loved to talk and put each other down. But it wasn't one-upmanship that kept the group together; it was our inordinate love for large quantities of booze.

The discussions were loud and lasted long into the night. The subjects were varied: politics, women, sports, music. To a man, we held Sinatra in the highest esteem. In a saloon, who but the world's greatest saloon singer would be considered patron saint? Looking back, I'm not sure why this scene was so intense. To some degree, it was a matter of well-known writers letting off steam. Then again, it may have been a simple case of scribes who preferred drinking to writing.

The drinking bouts at Elaine's went on for years. I can't remember the verbal encounters in any depth, but I do remember the most spectacular physical encounter: it was Leiber vs. Mailer, winner take all.

It began when Mailer walked into Elaine's with Buzz Farber. Mailer had a reputation for provoking people into fights and then letting Buzz, his tough-guy best friend, pulverize them. It was a routine they had perfected over several years. I had always ignored them, although once, out of loyalty to the Elaine's fraternity, I had helped Buzz by convincing a high-ranking exec at CBS to hire him to do a bullfight documentary in Spain. Buzz had returned from Spain with three reels of exposed film and a pseudo-Spanish accent. Although he had acted in some of Mailer's avant-garde movies, Buzz's attempt to direct had been a disaster. He was embarrassed to face me—knowing that I knew how he had messed up—and he was drunk. Rather than own up to the truth, he altered the truth.

He pointed to me and told Mailer, "This is the son of a bitch who did me out of a job. Who are you fucking over these days, Leiber?"

I ignored him, returning to the conversation with my friends.

"You're a coward."

"I am," I agreed.

"I can break your scrawny ass in half," Buzz asserted.

"Maybe you can."

"I'll bet you a thousand dollars I can break your arm in an arm-wrestling match. I'll snap it in two and shove it up your ass."

I considered the offer. Buzz was bulky and big. I was small. I weighed no more than 138, but, as a former gymnast and wrestler, I had maintained my strength. I was wiry and flexible. I thought I could take him and said so.

Sensing trouble, our hostess came over. Elaine wanted to make sure this didn't get out of hand. She agreed to referee and counted off. A fraction of a second after she said "three," I went for it and pinned him—just like that.

"Fuckin' cheater!" Buzz screamed.

"Where's the thousand dollars?" I asked.

He didn't pay up, but, rather than prolong the ordeal, I left him alone.

Buzz and Mailer retreated to a table. Meanwhile, I joined my friend Terry Southern. I ordered another drink, enjoying this significant triumph in an arena where male competition was always the subtext. I was tilted back, balancing my chair by putting my feet against the wall, when I felt an arm around my neck. At first I thought it a joke, but it didn't take long to realize someone was choking me to death. I couldn't breathe. I reacted by pushing my feet against the wall so violently that I kicked a hole in it. I figured my assailant was sore loser Buzz. But it wasn't. It was Mailer who had attacked, Mailer who was choking me. Elio the bartender rushed to my aid. He put his thumbs in Mailer's eyes.

"Let go of Leiber," he said, "or I'll blind you."

Mailer let go.

The onlookers applauded and roared with delight.

Another exciting night at Elaine's.

Stoller Another exciting date with Corky.

On this particular night we went to the Paris Theater, an art house that showed foreign films on Fifty-eighth Street across from the Plaza Hotel. The film was *A Man and a Woman,* Claude Lelouch's romantic melodrama.

Sitting there next to Corky, holding her hand, responding to the film's lush music, I definitely felt myself falling. But at this moment of my life falling in love wasn't what I wanted to do. And although the heat emanating from this new relationship could not be denied, I tried to keep my distance.

Leiber I loved Gaby, Gaby loved me, and yet our love life was anything but smooth. I blame myself. Gaby was always Gaby— a brilliant gal whose appreciation of life was inspiring. She was a dedicated mom to our boys and a dedicated lover of the arts. She

was a true highbrow who brought me into a refined ambience I never before knew. I should have been more appreciative. I should have been more loyal. I should have been home more. I should have been a lot of things. But instead I was hanging out at Elaine's.

Gaby tended to sleep late in the mornings. By the time she woke, I was already having breakfast at the Stage Deli on Seventh Avenue with Harold Clurman, the great theater innovator and director. We'd bullshit for thirty minutes or so, enjoying the flavor of the joint— the smell of pickles and hot pastrami and the presence of its owner, Max Asnas. Max was a Russian Jew who spoke the King's Yiddish. He brought back memories of my Baltimore childhood among my own immigrant relatives. Max could be crude and rude, but that was part of the fun. He also understood marketing. He knew that if he catered to the showbiz crowd, the showbiz crowd would be loyal to him. And they were. On any good day, you'd see Milton Berle or Henny Youngman or Myron Cohen or Fat Jack Leonard. You'd also often see an assortment of hookers. I loved the Stage.

My dish was chopped herring and a bagel. My reading matter was *Variety*. My mood was always serene as I took the corner table. Max liked me because he knew I was in "the business." Then when "the business" started to dissipate and midtown was taken over by tourists, Max wasn't happy. Max became passive-aggressive.

Max's frustration came to a climax on a morning when a group of female conventioneers from the Midwest marched into the Stage and took a table next to me and Clurman. Max saw how disturbed they were when they learned he did not serve blueberry muffins.

"Ladies," he said, "dis here is a deli. Not a tea party."

Unperturbed, they ordered tea and white toast. Max was unhappy. At one point he came over to join me and Clurman. In a loud voice, he asked the question that was heard from one end of the restaurant to the other.

"Vy do they call a pussy a cunt?"

The ladies at the next table gasped. They couldn't believe their ears.

"For God's sake, Max!" Harold Clurman retorted, putting his finger over his lips, "lower your voice."

"I should lower my voice in my own restaurant? In my own restaurant I say vhat I vant. So I'm asking you two geniuses a question. Vy do they call a pussy a cunt?"

"Why?" I asked, seeing that the ladies, despite their shock, were waiting for his answer.

"Because it looks like vun."

Eventually, though, the joke was on Max. The more he tried to alienate the tourists who frequented the Stage, the more they came. The Stage turned into a kind of Disneyland Deli of Seventh Avenue, and by the end of the sixties Max sold out.

24

A New Era

Stoller The new era had roots in the old era. The old era—
the fifties and early sixties, when we were writing and producing
rhythm & blues and rock and roll—stopped for us when we sold our
record company.

Prior to that, though, we got involved with Peggy Lee.

Leiber Of all those canaries that sang with the big bands
in the forties, outside of Billie Holiday, Peggy was the preeminent
nightingale. She'd sung with Goodman and later hit with novelty
tunes like "Mañana" and brilliant reinventions like her take on Rodgers and Hart's "Lover." In the fifties, she had a hit with "Fever."
She was also a superb writer; listen to the songs she created for the
Disney animated feature *Lady and the Tramp*, not to mention "It's
a Good Day" and "I Love Being Here with You." Peggy knew her
music. Her stylistic flexibility let her handle materials in virtually

every genre. So when Mike and I wrote a song we saw as an answer to Muddy Waters's "Mannish Boy" and Bo Diddley's "I'm a Man," we called it "I'm a Woman" and thought of Peggy, the funkiest white woman alive.

Stoller

The groove had a chantlike feel, and Jerry's words caught the can-do spirit perfectly:

> If you come to me sickly, you know I'm gonna
>   make you well
> If you come to me hexed up, you know I'm gonna
>   break the spell
> If you come to me hungry, you know I'll fill you
>   full o' grits
> If it's lovin' you're lackin', I'll kiss ya and give ya
>   the shiverin' fits
> 'Cause I'm a woman—W. O. M. A. N.
> I got a twenty-dollar gold piece says there ain't
>   nothing I can't do
> I can make a dress out of a feedbag an' I can make
>   a man out of you

We cut a demo in a little studio in the Brill Building and sent it to Dave Cavanaugh, Peggy's A&R man at Capitol. No response. Months passed. By chance I picked up the *New Yorker* and noticed an item about Peggy Lee at Basin Street East. Benny Carter was her conductor and, according to the reviewer, the highlight of her show was "I'm a Woman." I figured it had to be a different song with the same title, but on the slim chance that it was our tune I went to see her.

It was freezing cold and the streets were covered with ice. I barely managed to make my way to the club where, halfway through the show, she sang the song Jerry and I had written, "I'm a Woman." She hadn't changed a word or a note.

After the show, I waited outside her dressing room.

Twenty minutes later, I was ushered in. Naturally, I was nervous. After all, this was Peggy Lee. I explained that I had co-written "I'm a Woman." "Wonderful job," she said sweetly. "Lovely song." And that was it.

Next morning I called Cavanaugh. A little flustered, he explained that Peggy did indeed like the song and would soon record it, using only a rhythm section, as she had done it in her live show.

"How about a little more instrumentation," I urged. "How about a trumpet and a sax?"

Cavanaugh said, "Okay, that won't cost too much." We were invited to the session at Capitol's New York studios. We wound up contributing quite a bit. I wrote a horn chart, voicing the alto sax above the trumpet, something I took from Ray Charles's bag of arranging tricks. Jerry concentrated on the vocal interpretation.

Leiber I really didn't like the way she sang it, but there wasn't much I could do. I immediately saw that you could only push this gal so far. Her interpretation was too correct. She didn't play with the rhythm in the manner of Billie Holiday, one of her heroines. She simply sat on the beat. I didn't get it.

Stoller I got it. The public got it. "I'm a Woman" was an across-the-board hit and put Peggy back in business. It even nabbed a Grammy nomination. We never once received a call from Cavanaugh to congratulate us.

Years later, jazz musician Mike Melvoin told me that on his first day as Peggy's pianist, he was handed a stack of demos and told to pick out anything good. The only thing he liked was "I'm a Woman."

Leiber An interesting fact is that "I'm a Woman" hit in the middle of the girl group phenomenon and yet wasn't written about or sung by a girl at all, much less a teenage girl. If you look at the second verse, for example—

Feed the baby, grease the car an' powder my face at the same time
Get all dressed up, go out an' swing till four a.m. and then
Lay down at five, jump up at six an' start all over again

—it's clear that this wasn't written for a teenager. It was, in short, a feminist anthem that not only bucked the girl group trend. Its success was nothing short of remarkable. We had a hit with the great Peggy Lee. Which was why we were certain that she would soon be calling us for more tunes.

Never happened.

Stoller Peggy was a woman given to extreme moods. There were times when she treated us with great respect and expressed even greater gratitude. Other times we'd go to the studio to discover that we were in the doghouse. "I don't want Mike in here working with me today," she'd say. Or, "I don't want Jerry." No explanations were given. No explanations were needed. After all, she was Peggy Lee.

Leiber The decade rolled on. The decade got crazier. Assassinations. War. Cultural chaos. As I grew less interested in the teeny-bop sound of pop music, I found myself reading writers I'd never read before. Thomas Mann was one. Gaby introduced me to his work and pointed out one piece of short fiction in particular: "Disillusionment." The story fascinated me. It motivated me to look deep into the existential hole that sits in the center of our souls. It also inspired me to write a series of loosely connected verses in which I envisioned a character, a disillusioned woman, speaking, not singing, words to this effect:

> *I remember when I was a little girl our house caught on fire*
> *I'll never forget the look on my father's face*
> *As he gathered me up in his arms*
> *And raced through the burning building out onto the pavement*
> *I stood there shivering in my pajamas*
> *And watched the whole world go up in flames*
> *And when it was all over, I said to myself . . .*
> *"Is that all there is to a fire?"*

The second verse centered on the circus. As exciting as the greatest show on earth might have been, it left our narrator with the same question. The third verse was about a love affair gone wrong, and the fourth verse focused on what I called the "final disappointment."

Stoller   Jerry and I had been talking about stretching out as writers, and when he gave me these verses I saw this as the perfect vehicle to do just that. Jerry's vignettes ached with the bittersweet irony of the German cabaret. I wrote music that I hoped caught the spirit of Kurt Weill and Bertolt Brecht.

Then we got a call from Hilly Elkins, who was managing Georgia Brown. The English singer-actress known for "As Long as He Needs Me" was finishing her Broadway run of *Oliver!* and heading back to London for a TV special. She needed a song. When she heard those vignettes, she was convinced that that was it—except for one thing.

"It needs a chorus," she said, "something for me to sing between verses. The spoken parts are beautiful, but it needs something else."

Jerry and I agreed. We happened to have a chorus lying around, a leftover section from another song that didn't work. It came complete with lyrics. We played it for Georgia, and she loved it.

Leiber   When Georgia left, we looked at each other and agreed that the chorus made no sense. It contained the line, "They all wear coats with the very same lining and they pass bank notes on the seventh day." Obviously, this had nothing to do with the idea in the vignettes.

Mike said, "I'll go home and work on some music."

And I said, "I'll work on some lyrics."

The words came quickly to me:

> *Is that all there is?*
> *Is that all there is?*
> *If that's all there is, my friends,*
> *Then let's keep dancing*

Let's break out the booze and have a ball
If that's all there is

Mike called the next morning. "I've got the music. I wanna come over and play it for you."

When he arrived, I said, "Let me read you these words."

"Let me play you the music first," Mike said.

"Okay, Mike, play me what you wrote."

When he was finished, I said, "Play it again."

As Mike played, I sang and, miracle of miracles, the words and music fit perfectly together! In a long lifetime of collaborating, this has never happened before or since.

Georgia was delighted, and we all flew off to England, where her TV special was a great success.

Stoller Georgia performed "Is That All There Is?" but the BBC didn't record it. We wanted a record of the song interpreted by someone who understood this genre. We discussed Kurt Weill's wife, Lotte Lenya. Jerry also mentioned Claire Waldoff, an actress with the Berliner Ensemble. But a record company would never go for anyone that esoteric—not a record company in America anyway. The more we talked, the more it seemed the ideal candidate might be Marlene Dietrich. She certainly had the attitude. But the problem was, how to get to her?

Leiber I had an idea: Burt Bacharach. Burt had been signed to a new publishing company owned by Burt, his partner, Hal David, and me and Mike. Burt had also been Marlene's conductor. Maybe he could hook me up.

"Be happy to," he said. "Besides, it sounds like it was written in the thirties—the decade of Marlene's artistic glory."

Burt set it up. Even more graciously, he agreed to accompany me to Ms. Dietrich's apartment and play the song on her grand piano while I spoke-sang it.

Ms. Dietrich was in an expansive mood. Of course, the days of her luminous beauty were gone, but she was still well preserved and glamorous. She was keen on telling us all about her weekend in Hyannisport with the Kennedys. She exclaimed, "They are the closest that this country has to nobility. The extent of their cultural reach is truly impressive, and I could spend the rest of my life just listening to these charming people." It seemed like we were going to have to spend the rest of the evening hearing her go on about the famous Kennedy charm.

"Are you hungry?" she finally asked.

I was starved, and eager to see what delicacies would be brought forth. After all, Marlene Dietrich had a reputation as a master chef.

An elderly butler came in with a tray of stale hors d'oeuvres.

"A glass of wine?" she offered.

I accepted, hoping that some vintage white wine would make the cheese and crackers go down easier. But the Liebfraumilch was far too sweet for my taste.

After twenty more minutes of Kennedy worship, Burt gently reminded Ms. Dietrich why we were there.

"Of course," she said. "You boys have brought me a song. How delightful!"

Burt played it and I sang it.

The great star just sat there in silence. When she finally spoke, it was in the form of a question.

"Have you ever seen me perform, Mr. Leiber?"

For a second, I thought of lying. But then again, a lie might necessarily lead to other lies. Better be truthful. "I'm afraid I haven't, Miss Dietrich," I said.

"That must be true," she said. "If you had claimed to have seen me, I'd know you were lying. And the reason I'd know is because if you had seen me perform you would understand this simple fact: That song you just sang is who I am, not what I do."

Stoller "How about Streisand?" I asked Jerry.

"Streisand could sing it. Streisand's an actress. Let's send it to her."

I sent it to Streisand's manager. No reply ever came.

(Incidentally, when Streisand finally heard the song years later, she wanted to know why it had not been offered to her.)

Leiber "How about Peggy Lee?" I asked Mike. "This song has Peggy written all over it."

"After 'I'm a Woman,'" said Mike, "you'd think she'd show some interest in our stuff. But she never has."

"All we can do is keep trying."

When I learned that Peggy was in New York, I headed over to the Copa, where she was appearing. At a post-performance party, I handed her the demo and told her that I thought that the song was right for her. A week later she called back and said, 'I will kill you if you give this song to anyone but me. This is my song. This is the story of my life.'"

Bingo.

Stoller

We went to LA to have our initial meeting with Peggy at her home on Tower Grove. She wanted us to hear a debut album by a musician she liked: Randy Newman. Jerry and I loved Newman's work and thought it would be a great idea if he did the chart for "Is That All There Is?" We heard in Randy's work an irony and theatricality that we thought appropriate for our song. We were right. Randy's contributions went beyond the scope of what arrangers and orchestrators normally do. I'll be forever grateful to him.

25

Take 36

Leiber It was January of 1969 when we finally went into the studio with Peggy. We had a reputation as demanding producers, so Peggy set the rules from the start.

"I'll do three takes," she said, "and no more."

"That's cool, baby," I told Peggy, who arrived looking glamorous enough for her close-up. Black silk dress, full makeup, high heels.

As she walked to the mic, she was carrying a leather case that held a fifth of brandy that she placed close by.

The initial takes weren't great. She had to ease her way into the mood and find that sweet spot. At take 10, she still didn't have it. But being a trouper, Peggy kept going. At take 15, I suspect she took a belt because her readings were improving. Take 30 was good, but take 36 was pure magic. I looked at Mike and Mike looked at me and we could do nothing but jump up and down with joy. This was one of the greatest performances ever. Peggy had done it. We had done it. The enormous potential in this strange little song had been realized.

"Let's hear it back," I told the engineer.

We waited. Silence. We waited a little longer. More silence.

"What's wrong?" asked Peggy. "I'm dying to hear that last take."

Then came the words that cut through me like a knife. "I forgot to hit the record button," said the engineer.

"What do you mean you forgot to hit the record button?" I screamed at the top of my lungs. "This has to be a fuckin' prank! No one forgets to hit the record button. This was the greatest take in the history of takes! Stop joking! Let's hear it! Play the goddamn thing!"

But there was nothing to play. Nothing to do. Nothing had been recorded. Killing this kid would have been too kind. Yet Peggy, bless her heart, was stoic. "Guess I'll just have to sing it again," she said bravely. And she did. Take 37 was nothing short of marvelous. That's the take the world knows today. She is melancholy, she is sultry, she is fatalistic, she is in tune, and she delivers the song with a wondrous sense of mystery. It is good—it is, in fact, very, very good—but is not, nor will it ever be, take 36.

Stoller We'll always wonder how much bigger the song might have been had that miraculous take gone out over the airwaves. Meanwhile, it didn't look like take 37 would go out at all. Capitol refused to release it. For some reason, they didn't like it. At that point in her career Peggy wasn't selling records, and this new one—this existential treatise—was hardly what the company wanted to hear.

The company wanted to promote some of its new acts and hoped to get them on Joey Bishop's late-night TV show. Joey wasn't that interested in those artists, but agreed to host them if he could also get Peggy. Always cagey, Peggy saw her chance. "I'll go on the Bishop show," she said, "if you release 'Is That All There Is?' because that's the song I'm singing on the show."

Capitol capitulated. They pressed up some 1,500 copies of the 45 and Peggy gave a brilliant performance on national television. The minute she took her bow and Joey kissed her cheek, the phones start ringing—and ringing—and ringing some more. The first pressing sold out within hours. Within days the song was being requested from coast to coast. Within months it was climbing up the charts, where it remained. In 1969, the year of the Beatles' "Get Back" and "Come Together," the Stones' "Honky Tonk Women," Elvis's "Suspicious Minds" and Sly and the Family Stone's "Everyday People," "Is That All There Is?" became a sensation—the biggest in Peggy's long career—and a permanent part of the Great American Songbook.

From now on, Peggy would have to understand just how deeply we understood her artistry. With our songs and her singing our songs, there was no telling how far this collaboration could go.

Leiber

It went nowhere. Flush with success, Peggy decided that, although "Is That All There Is?" was an anomaly in the musical culture of the late sixties, she could be current. In order to be current, she started singing covers of the Beatles and Aretha Franklin that, to my mind, had nothing to do with her style.

After "Is That All There Is?" hit, I remember Peggy telling me that she was convinced that, in some spiritual realm, I had channeled her subconscious mind. Naturally, I just listened to her, but what I wanted to say, and didn't, was that she had actually blown the last line, which indicated to me that, on the deepest level, she really didn't understand the song. The lyric reads, "I'm in no hurry for that final disappointment." But Peggy said, "I'm *not ready* for that final disappointment." Back in the studio, I didn't have the heart to tell her that, especially after the lost take. But the key to the song is in the concept of redemption. And that final line—"I'm in no hurry"—is, in fact, a joke. I mean, who *is* in a hurry for the final disappointment? Not being ready connotes a far more somber attitude and misses the irony.

But whatever you might say about Peggy, she was a smart dame and a brilliant singer and, for all the travails, the song got over and gave her new life.

Stoller Just as we had thought Peggy would come back to us for more material after she'd hit with "I'm a Woman," we were certain she'd ask us for more songs after "Is That All There Is?" And just as we were wrong the first time, we were wrong this time as well. In spite of the unexpected success of "Is That All There Is?" Peggy showed no keen interest in working with us again. Her mercurial temperament combined with her inscrutable career strategy made her an even deeper mystery to us. She went her way and we went ours, but fate would eventually reunite us for the most extravagant musical venture of all.

26

Romance and Finance

Stoller I knew Corky was the one, and yet . . .

I resisted commitment like a bebopper resisting Lawrence Welk.
But Corky was irresistible. And she was everywhere. She played
piano in Clark Terry's big band; she played harp for Tony Bennett;
without acting the part, she was one of the hippest chicks in New
York City. Yet I was still playing the field. I remember going to a
party with Corky at the apartment of a sculptor and unexpectedly
encountering two other women with whom I had been a bit more
than friends. To say the least, it was awkward.

Corky got fed up. When her mother told her to "leave that guy
alone," Corky did just that.

"We're through," she announced when I came to see her. With
those words, she handed me a shopping bag containing the clothing
I kept at her place.

I was shocked and I was saddened.

"Can't we talk about it?" I asked.

"There's nothing to discuss," she said.

I left but did not give up. I kept calling.

"Can't we just have a drink?"

"No."

"Just one?"

"No."

Corky was adamant, but I was determined. A deluge of calls finally convinced her to meet me at Trader Vic's. I came equipped with an apology and a gift. The gift made her laugh.

"Oh, it's a snake ring," she said, "because you've been such a snake."

"Exactly," I confirmed, feeling both contrite and confident. After all, I was wearing my new Nehru suit.

I slowly worked my way out of the snake pit back into her heart. She moved in with me—permanently, that very evening. It was September of 1968.

Two years after that, I realized my commitment to noncommitment had more to do with fear than anything else. I proposed, Corky accepted, we sailed off to Europe on the *QE2* and have been happily married ever since.

Leiber   My sixteen-year marriage to Gaby Rodgers ended during the summertime in East Hampton. It was the early seventies. Looking back, I see my foolishness. At the time, I lacked the clarity to salvage what was clearly a beautiful romantic relationship. I could blame it on booze because everyone knew I was a world-class drinker. I could blame it on a distinct emotional immaturity. I could blame it on the personality of a guy in search of something that might not even exist. Maybe the entire concept of blame doesn't apply. Maybe Gaby and I were simply meant to meet, have our wonderful boys, have some wonderful years, and then go our separate ways.

My way continued to be somewhat crazy. There was, for example, this incident, this singular dinner party that led to my next romantic entanglement:

I was not with Gaby when Robert Motherwell and his wife, Helen Frankenthaler, invited me to their country home. It was an afternoon affair, and I remember that Bill de Kooning was there as well. I was seated next to a woman whose brilliance had a sexual edge that I found exciting. This was the famous Barbara Rose. I say famous because her essays on the very painters with whom we were dining had gained her a reputation. Clement Greenberg and Meyer Schapiro were the deans of the art critics, but Barbara was on her way up. And when it came to abstract expressionism, she knew everyone and everything about it. She told me that she came from my territory, a small town just north of Baltimore. I regaled her with stories of the music business, and she regaled me with stories of the art world. Just after the main course, she said, referring to Motherwell, "Let me take you downstairs, Jerry, and show you some of Bob's new work. Do you mind, Bob?"

"Not at all," said Bob, "you understand them more than I do."

Barbara led me to the basement. I walked behind, noting the swing of her hips and the shape of her sexy backside.

"I want to tell you why I think Bob's new work is so important," she said as we reached the bottom of the stairs.

But instead of talking, we started smooching and found our way to the laundry room, where we closed the door and squeezed inside.

Thus began our torrid affair.

Was I intrigued?

Of course.

In love?

Who knows?
In lust?
Most definitely.
Incapable of staying away from this hot tomato of an art critic?
Yes, yes, yes.

Stoller
The great shift in our professional lives had to do with dropping our aspirations as record company owners and fully embracing our gifts as songwriters. Along with that came a keener interest in accumulating copyrights, not simply our own but others as well. In the early seventies, we had been around for more than twenty years. We understood what the music business was all about. We saw that artists can—and will—come and go. The same applies to studio techniques and production styles. The one constant, though, was the song. The song remains. The song survives. And ownership of the song is the basis of permanent security. We wanted that sort of security. Beyond protecting copyrights of our own songs, we aggressively shopped for other catalogues that seemed to have permanent value. In a venture with Freddy Bienstock, we were successful in acquiring the scores to Broadway shows such as *Cabaret, Fiddler on the Roof,* and *Godspell,* rock and soul tunes like "The Twist," "Fever," "Good Lovin'," "Do You Believe in Magic," "I Got You (I Feel Good)," "Happy Together," and "Chantilly Lace," plus standards from the Great American Songbook like "April Showers," "Body and Soul," and "The Very Thought of You."

Those purchases relieved the pressure of being forced to write hits to make a living. At the same time, any songwriter who tells you he doesn't obsess about writing another hit is lying.

Leiber

Early in the seventies we produced the hit debut album of a new group, Stealers Wheel. The album went Top Ten in the US and the UK. Some saw Stealers Wheel, featuring Gerry Rafferty and Joe Egan, as an English version of Crosby, Stills, Nash and Young. Mike and I liked their harmonies and their open-minded, open-hearted approach to making music—not to mention the cases of Newcastle Brown Ale and Scotch whiskey that were consumed in great quantities. The album contained the smash single "Stuck in the Middle with You." Living in London and working at Apple, the Beatles' studio on Savile Row, was a blast. When we learned that George

Mike and Jerry at the Stealers Wheel session, Apple Studios, Savile Row, London, 1972.

Harrison wanted to come and use the facilities, I was happy to take off and fly to Rome for as long as George needed to work.

On the heels of our hit with Stealers Wheel, Procol Harum, the English group who had struck it rich with "Whiter Shade of Pale," called to see if we would produce them. Why not? We enjoyed our new status as senior advisers to British bands. They'd booked time at Ramport, the studio owned by the Who. The record was 1975's *Procol's Ninth*. The single, "Pandora's Box," charted in the UK. In fact, it was Procol's last hit. The album, which received strong reviews, included a nice cover of a song of ours that had been sung by Chuck Jackson in the sixties, "I Keep Forgettin'." In the eighties, Michael McDonald would launch his solo career with "I Keep Forgettin'," a song uncannily similar to ours. We all wound up sharing credit on his record.

Stoller In the seventies we enjoyed still another big hit in England, Elkie Brooks's "Pearl's a Singer," which we wrote with Ralph Dino and John Sembello. It's a poignant portrait of a singer "who stands up when she plays the piano" and who "sings songs for the lost and the lonely."

Our days and nights in London were lovely. When we made it clear that we preferred to work four-day weeks and enjoy long weekends, the artists were only too willing. When we arrived back from Sweden, France, or Morocco, the passport clerks would look at my papers and say, "If you're Stoller, where's Leiber?" Similarly, passing through customs, Jerry would get, "If you're Leiber, where's Stoller?" Somehow we became minor celebrities in the UK.

Back in the USA, though, our long-languished dream to write and produce a full suite of songs for Peggy Lee was finally going to be realized.

27

Mirrors

Stoller Zoot Sims once called Stan Getz "a great bunch of guys." Similarly, I could say that Peggy Lee was "a nice bunch of gals." And the word *nice* is accurate. But included in that bunch were an impatient gal, an imperious gal, a controlling gal, a volatile gal, and a gal shrouded in deep and impenetrable mystery.

Yet that bunch of gals had come back to us—or we had come back to her. Depends how you look at it. Either way, by 1975 we had compiled a suite of songs that were absolutely perfect for Peggy Lee. They represented exactly the kind of mature material that interested us most: songs rooted in mystery, offbeat humor, and dramatic irony. By then, though, Peggy Lee was no longer a diva in demand. She hadn't enjoyed a hit since "Is That All There Is?" had come out six years earlier. So low were her fortunes that Capitol had dropped her and left her without a label.

We went to A&M to see if we could help Peggy get a deal. In the mid-seventies, A&M was hot with hit acts like the Carpenters, the Captain and Tennille, and Cat Stevens.

Leiber

A&M Records was owned by Herb Alpert, the talented Tijuana Brass man, and Jerry Moss, a high-powered record promoter and businessman.

Moss wasn't too excited about signing Peggy. But we had just produced an international hit for him, "Stuck in the Middle with You," and he was grateful for our work.

"Look," he said, "we'll sign Peggy for one album—if you guys guarantee that you'll produce it."

We immediately went to the studio and supervised a session with a rhythm section only—stuff that was easy for Peggy to do.

Stoller

The second session was much different. We had a full orchestra and brilliant arrangements by Johnny Mandel for two of the more unusual pieces. We were extremely pleased with the results.

A meeting was called to discuss the project with Jerry Moss, Gil Friesen, Bob Fead, and some of the other A&M honchos. We played a few of the rhythm tracks before switching to the orchestral ones, "A Little White Ship" and "The Case of M.J."

Leiber

Gil was quiet for a few minutes before saying, "The rhythm tracks are really fine. Typically Peggy. But those last two with the orchestra are most unusual. I doubt if they're commercial. They're too weird, but they're brilliant. It's truly great work. Do the rest of the album like that."

Peggy was up for it. She liked these new songs as much as Gil did. What could go wrong?

Stoller Everything.

At first Peggy found Jerry abrasive and refused to sing if he didn't leave the studio. That was tricky, since Jerry was focusing on her vocals. But because Jerry wanted the record completed, he accepted his banishment. A little while later, though, I made a remark—I can't even remember what it was—that angered Peggy. Suddenly, I was banned and Jerry was brought back in. This pattern continued for weeks.

Leiber Peggy's creative juices didn't start to flow until after she had vented her anger at someone. She had to have an object of scorn. She had to have a target. It really didn't matter who. After a while, neither Mike nor I took her temper tantrums seriously. If she threw us out, we'd leave, knowing damn well we'd be back in a day or two. The material was so powerful that not even Peggy's volatility could kill the spirit of those sessions. In fact, her volatility may have contributed.

Stoller The opening track of the finished LP was "Ready to Begin Again," with a sensational orchestration by Perry Botkin, Jr. The second track, "Some Cats Know," featured the great Ray Brown on bass and a string chart by Meco Monardo. But the greatest contribution to the album was the arranging and conducting of Johnny Mandel. His charts were nothing short of magnificent. They created the perfect settings for Peggy to prove that she could be as unique and important a cabaret singer as Edith Piaf or Jacques Brel.

Leiber In spite of her diva tantrums, Peggy knew what we were going for. It was a highly idiosyncratic and whimsical grouping of songs that looked at life from different points of view. No actress-singer could ask for anything more.

Stoller We felt that her performances were some of her best, and these songs among the finest we had ever written.

Leiber "Ready to Begin Again" was inspired by Manya, my mother, and it's about the life force that Mom embodied so powerfully. It was originally composed as an audition for a musical version of *The Madwoman of Chaillot*, the play by Jean Giraudoux. To sing it requires exactly the kind of bravery that Peggy possessed:

> *When my teeth are at rest in the glass by my bed*
> *And my hair lies somewhere in a drawer*
> *Then the world doesn't seem like a very nice place*
> *Not a very nice place anymore . . .*
> *But I put in my teeth and I put on my hair*
> *And a strange thing occurs when I do*
> *For my teeth start to feel like my very own teeth*
> *And my hair like my very own too*
> *And I'm ready to begin again*

From there we moved to the sexiest song on the album, "Some Cats Know." I got the line from an old Slappy White joke that ended with, "If a cat don't know, a cat don't know." Mike and I wrote it for a

musical based on the novel *One Hundred Dollar Misunderstanding*.
The musical never happened, but Peggy sure as hell made the song
happen. She understood the subject—the art of foreplay:

> *Some cats know how to stir up the feelin'*
> *They keep foolin' 'round*
> *Till you're halfway to the ceilin'*
> *Some cats know how to make the honey flow*
> *But if a cat don't know, a cat don't know*

"Tango" has a tragic subtext. It was inspired by the death of Ramon
Novarro, the great silent film actor. He was reportedly murdered
in his apartment in an incident involving rough trade in 1968. The
news haunted me as I thought about the baffling relationship between
eroticism and violence.

> *Oh, the tango is done with a thin black moustache*
> *A wide scarlet sash, black boots and a whip*
> *Oh, the tango is done with seafarin' trash*
> *Reelin' from hash, fresh off a ship*
> *Oh, the tango is done, it's a dangerous dance*
> *A treacherous step and if one should trip*
> *The frail body breaks with a snap and a twist*
> *And a gold watch slips onto a thick-tattooed wrist . . .*

Stoller I wanted the music of "Tango" to have the feeling of old Hollywood. At the time I wrote it, I had discovered the
work of Astor Piazzolla, the Argentine composer and creator of the
"nuevo tango," a jazz-informed update of that style.

Mirrors also reflects work I had done nearly twenty-five years earlier. In the fifties, while studying with composer Arthur Lange, I'd written something I called "Suite Allegro" for clarinet, bassoon, violin, and cello. Two of those motifs had apparently never left Jerry's mind. When we started assembling songs for Peggy, he asked me to play two of the themes from that suite. The lyric of the first, "A Little White Ship," was fashioned by Jerry long after he had met with Tennessee Williams. Jerry still hoped to turn *Camino Real* into a musical. The project never saw the light of day, but Jerry's words fit the mood of the music.

> *Passage to places that hold hidden treasure*
> *And passage to places of forbidden pleasure*
> *To dark and deep places you'll be safe and sound in*
> *To dark and deep places you'll never be found in*

From left: Mike, Peggy and Jerry, Mirrors *session, 1975.*

> *A voyage through the night,*
> *A voyage to the light of day.*

The other song that came from my "Suite Allegro" was "The Case of M.J."

Leiber I'd been reading Truman Capote's short narrative "Miriam," and, influenced by it, I wrote a little story to be sung over Mike's music. It remains enigmatic to me, although I feel that it touches upon poignant turning points in the early life of a woman. Peggy told me that she related, and she sang the song as if she herself had written it.

> *Mary Jane tried to run away*
> *Mary Jane has been naughty today*
> *She won't eat her peas*
> *She won't say "thank you" or "please"*
> *And she's made a mess of her pretty white dress*

Stoller I don't think you can categorize *Mirrors* as a single-themed concept album. It's too diverse for that. "Professor Hauptmann's Performing Dogs," for example, is out of left field, a kind of military march played by an old-time German band. Jerry's lyrics are a brilliant combination of allegory and slapstick humor.

> *Professor Hauptmann's performing dogs*
> *Professor Hauptmann's incredible dogs*

One rides a pony and carries a purse
One is on roller-skates dressed like a nurse
A dog in a derby is doing a dance
A mutt in red suspenders keeps on losing his pants

Leiber
Before we started *Mirrors*, I came to Mike and said, "I've got an assignment you're not going to like."

"What makes you think I've liked any of the other ones?" Mike asked.

"Here's a very short lyric based on haiku poetry."

"Read it to me."

"I remember / When you loved me / I lie on my bed / Hands under my head / And remember / When you loved me."

"What do you want to call it?" Mike said.

"'I Remember,'" I said.

The next day Mike had the music—elegant, sparse, touching. The next week Peggy sang it in the studio. Her performance was flawless.

Stoller
Throughout the sessions, in spite of her wondrous interpretations, Peggy couldn't contain her fits of anger. It wasn't booze, because she didn't drink during these sessions. She'd taken up Transcendental Meditation.

One day, she was especially enraged. The music copyist had messed up; he neglected to indicate all the sharps and flats on the piano part of "Tango." The hour delay drove Peggy crazy. "I need a break," she said. "I'm going to meditate. I'll be back in twenty minutes." We took this as a sign of maturity. While she was gone, we fixed the piano part. When she returned from her mind-quieting session, she was as mad as a hornet. We wondered if she'd spent those twenty minutes meditating about whether to kill Jerry or me.

Leiber   *Mirrors* did not change Peggy's career. It didn't change ours either. I guess our hope was that an entire album of "Is That All There Is?"–styled songs might result in another "Is That All There Is?"–style hit. But in the mid-seventies, disco was creeping up the charts along with Barry Manilow and Tony Orlando. There was no mass market for *Mirrors*, no Peggy Lee fan base big enough to make the record a commercial success, and faint interest on the part of critics.

If I sound defiant, well, I am defiant. *Mirrors* is an important piece of work.

Stoller   Years later, traveling in Europe, I discovered that certain cults had formed around *Mirrors*. In many countries I visited, I was known as half of the Leiber and Stoller team celebrated not for the Robins or the Coasters or the Drifters, not for Big Mama Thornton or Elvis or Ben E. King, but for having coauthored Peggy Lee's *Mirrors*. That acknowledgment meant a lot to me.

28

The Last Clean Shirt

Leiber Like Muddy Waters or John Lee Hooker, T-Bone Walker was the real deal. Bluesman Incarnate. Raw, real, tough as nails, soft as silk, bittersweet, and a master of the craft. When we got a chance to produce him in the seventies, we jumped at it. Commerce didn't enter into it. This was art for art's sake. These were our roots. We were honored.

Stoller B.B. King will be the first to tell you that T-Bone Walker is his main source, a brilliantly innovative instrumentalist who electrified the country blues as well as his guitar. He turned the blues urban, infused it with a jazz feeling, and influenced virtually every guitarist who followed.

In putting together a T-Bone album, we decided to do the full-tilt boogie. We got a big band, a small band, a string section, the Sweet Inspirations—the best backup singers in the business—and a roster of superstar jazz musicians that included Dizzy Gillespie, Gerry Mulligan, Herbie Mann, Zoot Sims, Al Cohn, and David "Fathead" Newman. We also invited two of the greatest blues pianists: Charles Brown (who twenty years earlier had sung one of our first R&B songs, "Hard Times") and that keyboard genius from New Orleans, James Booker.

Leiber In his early days, T-Bone played his guitar behind his back and even with his teeth. Jimi Hendrix had studied him closely. When we began our collaboration, *Very Rare*, however, T-Bone's glory years were a distant memory. He had recently been in a serious car accident. He was sixty-two. Two years later, he would die of pneumonia. We realized that this was his last hurrah. That's one of the reasons we poured heart and soul into the project. The key song to me was something we wrote with the New Orleans drummer Charles "Honeyman" Otis called "The Last Clean Shirt."

> *Some people said it was whiskey, some people said it was gin*
> *But I know the name of the policy man that did my brother in*
> *They put the last clean shirt on my poor brother Bill*
> *We found him in the backseat of an old abandoned Ford*
> *When I touched the hand of my brother Bill, it was stiff as the*
>   *running board . . .*
> *The preacher said he's gone, gone to a better world*
> *He done fought his last fight, he done loved his last girl*

Stoller T-Bone sang several of our songs—"Three Corn Patches," "Been Down So Long," "If You Don't Come Back," and a version of "Kansas City"—but we also had him interpreting material like Percy Mayfield's "Please Send Me Someone to Love" that perfectly fit his mood. There were classics—Guitar Slim's "Well, I Done Got Over It" and Memphis Slim's "Every Day I Have the Blues"—but nothing was as poignant as T-Bone's own anthem, "Stormy Monday," a five-star production with both James Booker and Charles Brown on keys while Mulligan blew baritone sax and T-Bone sang and played his heart out.

The track began with T-Bone talking. He started telling me how he came by his nickname. I was intrigued. Unbeknownst to T-Bone, I signaled the engineer to hit "record." Later Jerry and I edited the monologue, and T-Bone loved that we included it on the record.

Leiber You couldn't say that our heart was really in the record business anymore. In the seventies, we had some solid hits, especially the stuff with Stealers Wheel. We were hot in England. We did our cabaret record with Peggy, and we did our blues record with T-Bone. But our goal was to reach beyond the charts and write musicals that would satisfy our artistic needs.

The most exciting thing that popped up was an adaptation of Mordecai Richler's *The Apprenticeship of Duddy Kravitz*. It had been a successful novel in 1959 and a successful movie with Richard Dreyfuss in 1974. In the early eighties, we were contacted about doing it as a musical. Mike and I jumped at the idea. Duddy was a Canadian Sammy Glick. The story was Yiddish-inflected and full of the kind of humor I loved. We went right to work. One of our first efforts was "The Businessman's Song," my homage to the sort of salesman I've known since I was a kid:

> *They'll tell you that he came up from the bottom*
> *They'll tell you that he didn't finish school*
> *Diplomas and degrees, he never got 'em*
> *But they'll also tell you he's nobody's fool*
> *'Cause a business is a business*
> *And a boss is a boss*
> *And a profit is a profit*
> *And a loss is a loss*

Another song describes the kind of vacation every working-class Jewish man dreams of:

> *Take it from me, Hymie, listen to Morty*
> *Two weeks and you won't look a day over forty*
> *You wouldn't go crazy, you wouldn't get nervous*
> *The food is fantastic, there's nothing but service*
> *Your own private cottage, a cozy cabana*
> *Your own little houseboy flown in from Havana*
> *He'll mix you a drink made from rum and papaya*
> *Then there's this gal, Hymie, you gotta try her*
> *You'll get to Miami, I'll give you her number*
> *She'll beat you, she'll eat you, she'll teach you the rhumba*
> *She's got this machine, what they call electronic*
> *You know what I mean? It's the highest colonic*

Stoller

It's depressing when years of work result in nothing tangible. One of the problems we had with *Duddy* was that Mordecai really wasn't interested in musicals. He was busy working on a screenplay based on another of his novels. Nevertheless, because he knew hit musicals earned a lot of money, he wanted to write the book for *Duddy*. As brilliant a novelist as he was, his libretto for *Duddy* never worked. When it opened in Canada, *Maclean's* magazine said the songs were good, but the direction and the libretto needed a lot of work. The producer had booked a string of dates that he felt he couldn't cancel. That gave us no time to fix things. As a result, the show died a painful death. *Duddy* the musical never made it across the border.

If *Duddy* didn't work, we were convinced that *Oscar* would.

Corky had gone to see a movie called *The Trials of Oscar Wilde* with Peter Finch and James Mason. She absolutely loved it and even wrote down the name of the writer-director: Ken Hughes. A few months later, Ken Hughes wrote me a letter. He loved Peggy Lee's *Mirrors* and wanted me to compose the music for a show about Oscar Wilde.

Hughes sent me a draft of the book for the musical loosely based on his movie script, plus several song lyrics. The draft was rough and the lyrics weren't great. I recommended, of course, that we use Jerry. Ken flew in from California to meet with us in New York. We all got along famously, and Jerry and I started writing songs.

Leiber

I love the songs we wrote for *Oscar*. One of the first was simply called "Homosexuals." It was to be sung by Lord Queensbury, Oscar's homophobic nemesis and the father of Oscar's lover.

Homosexuals, oh, how I hate them, oh, how I loathe the bloody lot
Why don't they just exterminate them, exterminate them on the
*   spot?*
Pansies, poofs and fairies, Nancy boys and queers
The flotsam and the jetsam one finds floating 'round the piers
Of sodomites and pederasts there seems to be no end
Doing all those nasty things that God did not intend
Jesus, Mary, Joseph, Matthew, Mark and Luke
Chartreuse and puce and fuchsia, it's enough to make you puke
Homosexuals, how I detest them, the very word sticks in my craw
Why in hell don't they just arrest them? Well, isn't it against the
*   law?*
And of all those so-called gentlemen who really get me riled
The one whose very presence makes me feel the most defiled
Is that intellectual homosexual, Mr. Oscar Wilde.

Mike wrote an exquisite ballad for "The Love That Dare Not Speak
Its Name."

I'm haunted by a love that dare not speak its name
A ghost of a sigh keeps whispering, "For shame" . . .
These passions that we deny are too wild to tame,
And, like moths, we're doomed to fly into the candle's flame

Stoller Unfortunately, personality conflicts developed
between bookwriter and songwriters and suddenly what had begun
as an ideal collaboration ended up in squabbles and finally separation. But we still have the songs and continue to hope that someday
the show will be produced.

29

Life and Art

Leiber   After Barbara Rose and I married somewhere in the mid-seventies, we moved to Italy. We lived there on and off over several years without a permanent house. Barbara was part of a community of expatriates—painters, sculptors, and writers—who liked the light and the life of the Italian countryside. We found some lovely property near Orvieto in Umbria, where I became obsessed with building an authentic country house. I emphasize the word *authentic*. I wanted it to look the way it would have looked in Michelangelo's time. I pulled out archival records of the plans of Renaissance architects; I hired masons and builders who worked only with centuries-old methods; I insisted that the fireplace in the kitchen be big enough so you could stand up in it—because that's how fireplaces were built in the sixteenth century. I visited stone quarries that had been there since the Middle Ages. I gave the orders. But because Barbara spoke fluent Italian and I spoke three words, each having to do with the bathroom, she had to translate. After years and countless cross-Atlantic trips, the house got built.

Then our marriage fell apart.

A memoir is no place to speak unkindly of a female companion, especially someone like Barbara Rose, who was courageous enough to accept my proposal of marriage. In spite of the red-hot encounter that marked the beginning of our relationship, the heat didn't last. The lust didn't last. And the love, if there really was any to begin with, went away.

We fought. We screamed. We accused. In the early eighties, I became sick with serious heart disease. I thought that my frailty frightened Barbara, and she ran. I knew that reconciliation required a great deal of work, and I ran from that work. I had my pleasures. I had enough money. I had my smokes and I had my drinks.

Stoller Despite the fact that we did some of our best work and enjoyed some successes in the seventies and eighties, those decades were filled with professional frustration. We couldn't get a musical going, despite several valiant attempts. Our song royalties and publishing interests kept us going financially, and, like Jerry and Barbara, Corky and I spent a great deal of time in Italy and other parts of Europe. In fact, one day running around Rome, I actually ran into Jerry on the street. It was pure coincidence.

"I guess this proves it," said Jerry.

"Proves what?" I asked.

"We couldn't get away from each other if we tried."

We stopped and had an espresso. He told me that his marriage wasn't going well. Of course, I sympathized. I felt fortunate that in Corky I had found the right woman. I wished the same happiness for Jerry.

"I'll be happy when someone tells us Sinatra has recorded that song."

Jerry and Mike, 1988.

He was referring to a song called "The Girls I Never Kissed." We had written it with Frank in mind. Jerry's lyrics said,

> *The old wolf sniffs the summer breeze and dreams about*
>   *his youth*
> *For the sight of skirts above the knees turns his hardboiled*
>   *brain to cheese*
> *And the scent of honey in the trees whets an old sweet*
>   *tooth*
> *The pretty girls go strolling by, I look at them, and heave*
>   *a sigh*
> *And think of all the things I've missed, and all the pretty*
>   *girls I never kissed*

Leiber One day Mike and I were having lunch at the Friars Club in New York. At a nearby table sat a bunch of old-school music business guys. Among them was Frank Military, a classy song plugger whose specialty was finding tunes for Sinatra. Sinatra was known for flawless taste in songs, so you figured that Military knew his business.

"This business is driving me nuts," said Military, an elegant man who wore Oxxford suits, Turnbull and Asser shirts, and Ferragamo shoes.

I leaned over and asked, "Why is that?"

"No one gives a shit about songs anymore," said Frank. "They don't even call 'em songs. They call 'em 'product.' Producers ask, 'You got any product for me?' Next producer who calls a song 'product' gets my foot up his ass. In the old days, you could hang out at Luchow's and talk songs—real songs—with real songwriters. You could talk to Irving Berlin or Jerome Kern and actually discuss the meaning of a lyric. These days it's nothing but money, money, money. I can't even remember the last time I heard someone say, 'Frank, I have an absolutely gorgeous song that's actually intelligent and perfect for Sinatra.'"

"Frank," I said, "I have an absolutely gorgeous song that's actually intelligent and perfect for Sinatra."

"I don't believe you."

"It's already written," I said. "Mike and I custom-wrote it for Sinatra."

"What's it called?"

"'The Girls I Never Kissed.'"

"I like the title."

"You'll like the song. Sinatra will like the song."

"When can I hear it?"

"We'll do a demo and have it on your desk in two days."

"Don't wanna wait two days, Jerry. I want to hear it now."

"Fine. Come up to my place, and Mike and I will do it for you."

I lived within walking distance of the Friars Club.

Soon as we got there, we played it. Military loved it.

"Frank will eat it up," he said. "He'll kiss my ass in front of the fiddlers at Capitol Studio."

"Are you sure Sinatra will like it?"

"I promise."

Two weeks later Military called from California. "Frank's recording it," he said.

"When?"

"Next week."

Next week came and Military called. "Frank cut it," he said, "but it didn't work. I hate to tell you this, Jerry, but he didn't like the arrangement."

Mike and I were devastated.

Mike and I were elated when Military called the next day.

"Frank's decided to try again."

"Great!"

But then we learned that Frank never showed up for the second session. He wasn't in the mood.

Some time after that, I got a call from filmmaker Billy Friedkin inviting me to a Sinatra show at Carnegie Hall. I was reluctant to go.

"There's a full bar in the Carnegie Hall lobby," Friedkin said.

I went.

Sinatra was great. The band behind him was great. At the end of the show, standing in front of the rhythm section, Frank dismissed all the musicians except Bill Miller, his piano player. Then he said:

"We'd like to do a new song for you. I don't know it very well, but I'll do the best I can. It's a marvelous song written by a couple of kids who, strangely enough, used to write for Elvis Presley and do all those rock things and suddenly they grew older and now they write pretty songs, ballads, you know, not the 'Hound Dog' and 'Wolf Dog' and all those other 'Mother's Ass' things they used to do—stupid, goddamn songs. This, you might say, is reminiscent of a song like 'September Song.' Their names are, I think, Ron Leiber and Mike Stoller."

With that, Sinatra sang "The Girls I Never Kissed."

His voice wasn't in the best shape. He ate a couple of the lyrics. But fuck it all—he did the thing.

And here's the happy coda: Sinatra finally recorded it with a beautiful string arrangement by Billy May.

30

Smokey Joe's

Leiber By the late eighties, I was already living in LA when my third son, Jake, was born. I had had a romance with his mother, Nadia Ghaleb, which unfortunately did not last long. But our love for Jake has been steadfast and strong. Nadia has done a wonderful job raising him into a fine young man. I wasn't around as much as I would have liked. After an earthquake, Nadia was uneasy in California, and she and Jake moved to New York.

Stoller In 1989, we completed the circle. The Leiber-Stoller partnership had begun in LA. We had met as transplanted easterners who understood and loved the blues. We wrote our California blues from 1950 through 1957 until Ahmet and Wexler called us to Atlantic. We stayed in New York for three decades. The winters had finally gotten to us. We also weren't thrilled that our many attempts to get a musical on Broadway had been in vain. Other efforts like *The*

Jerry and Jake, 1993.

International Wrestling Match, songs we had written to turn an off-Broadway play—a Brechtian apocalyptic melodrama—into a musical, hadn't taken off. It seemed a good time to settle down into the setting of our initial success. We could use the relaxation. I found a panoramic view of LA attached to a house in the hills. Jerry had dreamed of building a house at the beach.

But just as we started to relax, something happened.

In the early eighties, two shows were mounted in London featuring all Leiber and Stoller songs. One, *Only in America*, was directed by Ned Sherrin, who had just done *Side by Side by Sondheim*. A couple of years later, *Yakety Yak* arrived in a little theater in the East End and subsequently moved to the West End for a three-month run. Both shows had less than stellar books.

Almost a decade later, a director in Seattle who headed a university drama department asked Jerry for the go-ahead to mount still another musical of Leiber and Stoller songs.

"We don't have the money to license the songs," the producer said.

"Go ahead anyway," said Jerry. "Who's gonna know?"

Variety knew. Their reviewer flew to Seattle and wrote a rave. When we read the accolades, Corky and I went to see for ourselves. The book still didn't work, but when the songs were sung and danced, the audience went wild. Something was definitely happening. I invited a couple of Broadway producers to Seattle, and they agreed with me. Lousy book, but amazing audience reaction to the songs.

I said, "Screw the book. Let's do the show with just the songs."

Then came a flurry of activities.

First, the producers hired a director who claimed to know more about us than we knew about ourselves. His workshop was so bad the project was shelved.

Next came a flashy choreographer. This guy was dead certain he knew how to do the show. He wanted Jerry to come to New York to help him put together a mini workshop. They did it in a week's time. I arrived the day before the presentation. That night a devastating blizzard hit New York. We figured no producers would show up, but they did. And they all liked it.

Leiber

The choreographer insisted on taking over. He not only wanted to direct, he wanted to write the book.

"Hell, no," I said. "Mike and I don't want a book. The songs are their own stories."

"But without a book, how can I address the problem of racism?"

"Hey, man, we know a lot about racism. Any number of our songs deal with racism in one way or another. But we're doing a good-time musical here, and we don't want any kind of book. We just want our songs staged, sung, and danced."

The tug-of-war went on into Chicago until the producers finally sidelined the choreographer. In Chicago the show was called *Baby, That's Rock and Roll*. We really didn't want "rock and roll" in the title. We didn't think all of our songs were rock and roll.

Things got more exciting when Jerry Zaks agreed to direct. Zaks had recently won Tonys for *Six Degrees of Separation* and *Guys and Dolls*. He was first-rate. He also agreed with us that no book was needed. And *Smokey Joe's Café: The Songs of Leiber and Stoller* was born.

Months of work, round-the-clock rehearsals. The songs were chosen. The cast was pitch-perfect, the choreography brilliant. It previewed in LA in 1994. We were certain we had a winner.

Stoller

Variety called it a loser. *Variety* fried it. The trade paper said, "Just buy a boxed set of Phil Spector records instead." The Phil Spector line was the lowest blow of all.

Smokey Joe's Café poster for the London production.

Leiber

Screw *Variety.*

Within a week, there was a line around the block every night, waiting to see if there were any cancellations. The reviewer hated it, but the people loved it. It moved to New York, ran for five years, and became the longest-running musical revue in Broadway history. It ran for two years in the West End in London; it's played in Japan, Australia, Brazil, and Turkey; it's toured Germany and Switzerland twice, and it's still enjoying road company productions in a dozen American cities.

Stoller

So we wound up on Broadway for a long stay, but not as we had planned. For all our concentrated efforts to write an original musical, it was our original songs that Broadway audiences—and, for that matter, audiences around the world—wanted to hear.

We remain certain that an original musical is still within our grasp. We're not giving up.

Leiber

I didn't give up on love. I met Tere Tereba, a hip and beautiful woman with an intriguing history with the Andy Warhol gang, Jim Morrison, and a host of others. She's been a fashion designer, an astute art collector, and has just written a book about Los Angeles gangsters. That she is now with a musical gangster—as someone once called me—is credit to her patience and fortitude.

My Greene and Greene–styled house on Venice Beach takes me back to not only the beginning of this book, but the beginning of my life.

Tere Tereba.

You might remember that a few hundred pages ago a grade-school teacher took me on a tour in Pasadena of the Gamble House, designed by Greene and Greene. This made an impression on me as the greatest example of Craftsman architecture. I swore that if I ever had the means, I would build a monument of my own dedicated to the Greene and Greene style. Well, the monument is built. It took four years. It took special builders and special materials; it took a singular vision to replicate the moldings and staircases, the thousands of details that give the place its signature aesthetic.

I sit here watching the endless parade of life on the promenade just outside my door. I have not tasted booze or had a cigarette in my mouth for many years now, which is surely why I'm still alive. As I watch the parade, I am sober. That fact does not make me especially happy. For me, sobriety can be dull. I think back to the days of cognac and tobacco with deep nostalgia. But, after a series of major heart operations, I cling to life. I peruse the erotic images of Helmut Newton and imagine an entire musical based on these images. Words come to mind. Music.

I go to work.

I take a break and think about my children: Jed, a great keyboard player, producer, and owner of a hot Hollywood recording studio; Oliver, who plays four instruments beautifully, and works as a successful record producer, songwriter, and arranger; and Jake, a brilliant student and champion sportsman.

I might have made more than a few messes in my love life, but I couldn't be more proud of my sons.

Stoller Our three-level house in the Hollywood hills has a view from downtown to the ocean. Corky and I each have our own office on a different level. It is a house filled with harps and pianos, paintings that we love, and tons of framed photos. A hardcore Democrat and political freedom fighter, Corky has rekindled my own interest in politics. We're activists, and we're out there on the front lines.

The Leiber-Stoller publishing catalogue, most of which was recently sold, was supervised, beginning in 1985, by Randy Poe, our friend and esteemed associate. Randy has worked tirelessly to protect our accumulated copyrights and advise us, with unerring accuracy, when to hold and when to fold. Thanks to Randy, we've managed to both acquire and liquidate valuable songs at just the right time.

From left: Oliver and Jed Leiber, Los Angeles, 2005.

My time is spent on new work. I'm working on a new musical. It's one of the few things I've done without Jerry, but Jerry and I continue to work on other projects.

When I'm not writing new songs or rewriting old ones, I can often be found playing poker at the Hollywood Park Casino or enjoying evenings with Corky and the many good friends we've made in LA.

All around my workroom at home there are many plaques referring to the honors that Jerry and I have received. When I'm working on a new song and can't come up with anything I'm happy with, glancing at the Songwriters Hall of Fame certificate reassures me. *Hell, if I did it before I can do it again.* I look at the acknowledgment

From left, Mike, President Clinton, and Jerry at the Oval office, 1993.

of our induction into the Rock and Roll Hall of Fame and remember the day of the ceremonies, when I said, "We never planned to write rock and roll. We just tried to write good rhythm & blues." And that's the truth.

I like looking at the photos of some of the people that Jerry and I worked with and admired. Unfortunately there are precious few if any photos of us with Charles Brown, Willie Mae Thornton, the Robins, the Coasters, Ruth Brown, Joe Turner, LaVern Baker, Little Willie Littlefield, Esther Phillips, Johnny Otis, Wynonie Harris, and Linda Hopkins. The reason is simple enough. No one thought anyone would care much about what we were doing back then. We were proud of our work but didn't have the slightest notion that those songs or records would be remembered three months later—or, unbelievably, fifty or more years later.

Sometimes I think back to the difficult times my dad had and the troubles faced by my mom, and realize how lucky I've been. Lucky that in spite of the hardships they endured, my parents' love gave me the capacity for happiness. Lucky to have met a seventeen-year-old named Jerry Leiber. Lucky to have Corky. Lucky to have survived in the often brutal business of music. Lucky to have three terrific children: my darling daughter Amy, who lives in New York, is a dialect coach working in the theater. She can teach a native of Bombay to sound like a native of Brooklyn and a Texan to sound like a Liverpudlian. My son Peter and his delightful and talented wife, Tricia, live in LA. Gifted in all things musical and literary, Peter looks after Jerry and me and our legacy. Adam resides near the town of

From left, Peter, Corky's mom, Dorothy; Corky; Adam; Mike; Amy; and Jimmy Witherspoon, 1985.

Wexford, Pennsylvania, with the wonderful Sharon Galli, a neonatal pediatrician. Adam is constantly traveling in his work as an independent consultant in the Internet world. His high-tech work is over my head, but I know he's superb at it.

I've used the word "lucky" a lot. But maybe the word isn't "lucky." Maybe the word is "blessed." And for those blessings, I'll always be grateful.

Mike and Jerry get their star on the Hollywood Walk of Fame, 1994.

Leiber Lately I've found myself schlepping from one doctor's office to another. Somehow, in spite of some formidable challenges, this body of mine has managed to keep going. I trust it will continue to do so for a while, but who knows?

If my next medical report is, "Leiber, you've run out of options. You've got a month at most to put your affairs in order," then this is my plan: I'm going to buy a fifth of Maker's Mark bourbon, a carton of Camels, and as many Billie Holiday records as I can carry. I'm going to break out the booze and have a ball.

If that's all there is.

Appendix A:
The Songs

by Randy Poe

With a little assist by a large black woman from Montgomery and a skinny white dude from Memphis, Leiber and Stoller practically invented rock and roll. You think I'm lyin'? Dig this.

Leiber and Stoller's earliest songs were recorded by blues acts like Jimmy Witherspoon, Little Esther, Amos Milburn, Charles Brown, Little Willie Littlefield, Bull Moose Jackson, Linda Hopkins, and Willie Mae "Big Mama" Thornton.

It was that first Big Mama Thornton record that went and changed everything. Although it was written in the standard blues form (first line/first line repeated/rhyming third line), "Hound Dog" was much more than just another blues song. Big Mama's recording—with Johnny Otis's unique drumbeat and Pete Lewis's gut-bucket guitar licks—was the forerunner to much of the R&B that followed immediately thereafter.

The moment Elvis heard Freddie Bell and the Bellboys' near-parody version of Big Mama's record a couple of years later, he knew he had to cut it. When Presley went into the studio, this time it was

D.J. Fontana's angry snare drum roll and Scotty Moore's machine-gun guitar solo (and, of course, that "take-a-hike, bitch" attitude in Elvis's vocal) that transformed "Hound Dog" from an R&B hit into a rock and roll standard. Hell, let's face it—it's *the* rock and roll standard. How could it be topped?

But the cool thing about Leiber and Stoller is that they kept on growing as songwriters. The blues and R&B were hip, and their early rock and roll tunes captured the kids' imaginations, but L&S had more to say—a lot more. Leiber slipped some serious shit into the lyrics of Coasters songs like "Along Came Jones" and "What About Us," while Stoller composed melodies and rhythms that far surpassed the I-IV-V chord progressions and 4/4 time signatures most of the other cats from that era were still hung up on.

In those days, it seemed like everybody with a record deal was getting into what Leiber and Stoller were laying down. The names of many of the artists who recorded L&S tunes in the fifties and sixties now line the walls of the Rock and Roll Hall of Fame. As a matter of fact, Leiber and Stoller are right there in that Hall with them, as well as the Songwriters Hall of Fame.

From the late sixties on, Jerry Leiber and Mike Stoller just kept moving forward—always three steps ahead of everyone else. Peggy Lee had already scored a hit with L&S's "I'm a Woman," but they had something a bit more serious in mind for her—the partly spoken, partly sung "Is That All There Is?"

According to music critic Robert Palmer, "'Is That All There Is?' clearly pointed to the direction Leiber and Stoller's new work would take." And it was this new direction that prompted Palmer to write, "The golden age of rock and roll had come to an end."

Like I said before, Leiber and Stoller practically invented rock and roll. But they'd said everything they had to say in the confines of that genre, so they chose to keep stretching out. There would be more songs for Peggy Lee, for Barbra Streisand, for Liza Minnelli, and even one—a great one—for Frank Sinatra.

But if new kids wanted to keep recording their older songs, that was okay, too.

Between 1950 and right now, damn near everybody has gotten in on the act: the Beatles, the Rolling Stones, B.B. King, James Brown, Little Richard, Jerry Lee Lewis, the Beach Boys, Buddy Holly, Ben E. King, Fats Domino, Jimi Hendrix, Buck Owens, Muddy Waters, Joe Williams, Trisha Yearwood, Tom Jones, George Jones, Count Basie, Edith Piaf, Eric Clapton, Willie Nelson, Johnny Mathis, Luther Vandross, Neil Diamond, John Lennon, Aretha Franklin, and hundreds more.

Despite everything, if they had written no other song but "Hound Dog," the names Leiber and Stoller would still have been indelibly written in the history of popular music. But Jerry Leiber and Mike Stoller's contributions to the world of songwriting have been so monumental that it is impossible to envision what American popular music would be like today without them.

The Chart Hits of Leiber & Stoller

This is the complete list of songs written or co-written by Jerry Leiber and/or Mike Stoller to reach the top 100 in the US or UK, listed alphabetically by title, with the artist and release date. All songs by Jerry Leiber and Mike Stoller unless otherwise indicated.

An asterisk (*) indicates a record produced by Leiber & Stoller.

TITLE	ARTIST	YEAR
"Along Came Jones"	The Coasters*	1959
	Ray Stevens	1969
"Bazoom (I Need Your Lovin')"	The Cheers*	1954
	Otis Williams & The Charms	1955

TITLE	ARTIST	YEAR
"The Best Thing" (Leiber, Stoller, Dino, Sembello)	Billy Eckstine	1976
"Black Denim Trousers and Motorcycle Boots"	The Cheers*	1955
	Vaughn Monroe	1955
"Bossa Nova Baby"	Elvis Presley	1963
"(How 'bout a Little Hand for) The Boys in the Band"	The Boys in the Band	1970
"Charlie Brown"	The Coasters*	1959
	The Compton Brothers	1970
"The Chicken and the Hawk (Up, Up and Away)"	Joe Turner	1955
"D. W. Washburn"	The Monkees	1968
"Dance with Me" (Leiber, Stoller, Lebish, Treadwell, Nahan)	The Drifters*	1959
	Rick James (as part of medley)	1989
"Dancin'"	Perry Como	1957
"Do Your Own Thing"	Brook Benton*	1968
"Don't"	Elvis Presley	1958
	Sandy Posey	1973
"Down Home Girl" (Leiber, Butler)	Old Crow Medicine Show	2006
"Down in Mexico"	The Coasters*	1956
"Drip Drop"	The Drifters*	1958
	Dion	1963
"Fools Fall in Love"	The Drifters*	1957
	Jacky Ward	1977
"Framed"	The Robins*	1954
"Get Him" (Leiber, Stoller, Russell, Passman)	The Exciters	1963
"The Girl Who Loved the Man Who Robbed the Bank at Santa Fe (And Got Away)" (Leiber, Stoller, Wheeler)	Hank Snow	1963

TITLE	ARTIST	YEAR
"Girls, Girls, Girls"	The Coasters*	1961
	The Fourmost (UK)	1965
"Hard Times"	Charles Brown	1951
"His Kiss" (Stoller, Russell)	Betty Harris	1964
"Hound Dog"	Willie Mae "Big Mama" Thornton*	1953
	Elvis Presley	1956
"I (Who Have Nothing)" (Mogol, Donida, Leiber, Stoller)	Ben E. King*	1963
	Terry Knight & The Pack	1967
	Tom Jones	1970
	Liquid Smoke	1970
	Sylvester	1979
"I Keep Forgettin'"	Chuck Jackson*	1962
"I Keep Forgettin' (Every Time You're Near)"	Michael McDonald	1982
"I Want to Do More"	Ruth Brown	1955
"I'll Be There" (Leiber, Stoller, King, Jones)	Damita Jo	1961
"I'm a Hog for You (Baby)"	The Coasters*	1959
"I'm a Woman"	Peggy Lee	1962
	Maria Muldaur	1975
	Jeanne Pruett	1978
"Idol with the Golden Head"	The Coasters*	1957
"Is That All There Is?"	Peggy Lee*	1969
"Jack-o-Diamonds"	Ruth Brown*	1959
"Jackson" (Leiber, Wheeler)	Johnny Cash & June Carter	1967
	Nancy Sinatra & Lee Hazlewood	1967
"Jailhouse Rock"	Elvis Presley	1957
"Just Tell Her Jim Said Hello"	Elvis Presley	1962

TITLE	ARTIST	YEAR
"Kansas City"	Wilbert Harrison	1959
	Rocky Olson	1959
	Hank Ballard	1959
	Little Richard	1959
	Trini Lopez	1964
	James Brown	1967
"King Creole"	Elvis Presley (UK)	1958
"Little Egypt"	The Coasters*	1961
"Lorelei"	Lonnie Donegan (UK)*	1960
"Love Me"	Elvis Presley	1956
"Love Potion #9"	The Clovers*	1959
	The Searchers	1965
	The Coasters*	1971
"Loving You"	Elvis Presley	1957
"Lucky Lips"	Ruth Brown*	1957
	Gale Storm	1957
	Cliff Richard	1963
"My Claire De Lune"	Steve Lawrence	1961
"On Broadway" (Leiber, Stoller, Mann, Weil)	The Drifters*	1963
	George Benson	1978
"One Kiss Led to Another"	The Coasters*	1956
"Only in America" (Leiber, Stoller, Mann, Weil)	Jay & The Americans*	1963
"Past, Present and Future" (Leiber, Butler, Morton)	The Shangri-Las	1966
"Pearl's a Singer" (Leiber, Stoller, Dino, Sembello)	Elkie Brooks (UK)*	1977
"Poison Ivy"	The Coasters*	1959
	Young & Restless	1990
"Rat Race" (Leiber, Stoller, McCoy)	The Drifters*	1963

TITLE	ARTIST	YEAR
"The Reverend Mr. Black" (Leiber, Stoller, Wheeler)	The Kingston Trio Johnny Cash	1963 1982
"Ruby Baby"	The Drifters Dion Billy "Crash" Craddock	1955 1963 1975
"Run Red Run"	The Coasters*	1959
"Santa Claus Is Back in Town"	Elvis Presley (UK)	1957
"Saved"	LaVern Baker*	1961
"Searchin'"	The Coasters* Jack Eubanks Ace Cannon	1957 1961 1964
"Shake 'em Up and Let 'em Roll"	Earl Richard George Kent	1968 1976
"She's Not You" (Leiber, Stoller, Pomus)	Elvis Presley	1962
"Shoppin' For Clothes" (Leiber, Stoller, Harris)	The Coasters*	1960
"Smokey Joe's Café"	The Robins*	1955
"Some Other Guy" (Leiber, Stoller, Barrett)	The Big Three (UK)	1963
"Spanish Harlem" (Leiber, Spector)	Ben E. King* King Curtis Aretha Franklin	1960 1966 1971
"Stand by Me" (Leiber, Stoller, King)	Ben E. King* Earl Grant Spyder Turner David & Jimmy Ruffin John Lennon Mickey Gilley Maurice White 4 The Cause	1961, 1986 1965 1967 1970 1975 1980 1985 1998
"There Goes My Baby" (Leiber, Stoller, Nelson, Patterson, Treadwell)	The Drifters* Donna Summer	1959 1984

TITLE	ARTIST	YEAR
"Treat Me Nice"	Elvis Presley	1957
"Trouble"	Gillan (UK)	1980
"Turtle Dovin'"	The Coasters*	1955
"What About Us"	The Coasters*	1959
"What to Do with Laurie" (Leiber, Stoller, Wheeler)	Mike Clifford*	1962
"(When She Wants Good Lovin') My Baby Comes to Me"	Chicago Loop	1966
"Yakety Yak"	The Coasters*	1958
	Eric Weissberg & Deliverance	1975
"Young Blood" (Leiber, Stoller, Pomus)	The Coasters*	1957
	Bad Company	1976
	Bruce Willis	1987
"(You're So Square) Baby I Don't Care"	Elvis Presley	1958
	Joni Mitchell	1982
"You're the Boss"	LaVern Baker & Jimmy Ricks*	1961

A complete list of issued Leiber & Stoller song recordings can be found at www.leiberstoller.com/Discography.html.

Appendix B:
The Productions

by Peter Stoller

"We didn't write songs; we wrote records."

Leiber and Stoller's most famous quote about their own work has haunted them for decades. The common inference has been that what they wrote weren't really songs. Of course, Leiber and Stoller did write songs—hundreds of them—and the thousands of recordings of those songs demonstrate how well they've held up. What Jerry and Mike meant was, they didn't *merely* write songs. Rather, they also conceived the entire record in their heads: the arrangement, the style, the sound, the nuances of the vocal performances. In short: the production.

Leiber and Stoller were part of the first generation to come of age hearing songs initially and primarily as records, both on radio broadcasts and record players: the song and the performance as one definitive creation. And, thanks to upheavals in the music industry and American society as a whole, a great many of those records were blues and R&B.

They didn't know it was production when they started. "Production" wasn't even a word anyone used with regard to recording. It was a term invented for Leiber and Stoller when they were negotiating with Atlantic to get a credit for making the records and the freedom to work for other labels, in what is now widely acknowledged as the world's first independent record production deal.

Prior to that, a staff artists & repertoire (A&R) man would match singer to song, and then supervise the session to make sure it was a good fit. Some A&R men were prodigiously talented and made excellent records, but they did it on salary or for a fee, and usually without an intimate understanding of the songwriter's intent. Sometimes, the bandleader would run the session, and sometimes that bandleader was also the songwriter. However, as a rule, he'd get no special credit for doing this, nor additional pay, and he didn't run sessions for other performers.

So Leiber and Stoller introduced two seemingly contradictory notions: first, that production was part of songwriting; and, second, that production was a separate job. The latter notion was a matter of their profession; the former, of their art.

Neither of these things was part of their original plan. Rather, as they've put it, "we became producers out of self-defense." Some of the earliest records of their songs failed to capture the sound they were hearing in their heads. When it came to "Hound Dog," with Big Mama Thornton not grasping the intent and Johnny Otis abdicating his drum stool to a less apt player, they had to take matters into their own hands. The results speak for themselves.

As early as 1954 and the Robins' "Riot in Cell Block #9," the totality of their conception is in evidence: the *Gang Busters* sound effects intro, the strip-joint choruses with their lurid sax breaks, the transformation of a preeminent "bird" group into a surly gang of hardened criminals, down to the drafting of Richard Berry for his note-perfect delivery as the lifer-cum-narrator. You can't notate those details on a lead sheet, nor explain them to an A&R man.

With the Coasters, Leiber and Stoller evolved their "playlet" form to dramatize virtually anything they found funny: the street-corner lotharios of "Young Blood," sharing their appreciation of youth in bloom with each other as much as with the listener; the dictatorial parents of "Yakety Yak," with mom-and-pop twin lead vocals and the titular yap of quasi-rebellious teens; the insipid (and oppressively white) television fare of "Along Came Jones," from the hammy melodrama to the hollow clip-clop of the laconic lawman's horse; and the full-blown production number that is "Little Egypt," complete with carnival barker, acrobatic exhibition, and "seven kids" singing "gitchy-gitchy." In each case, the production is equal partner to the melody and lyrics; "just the song" would be like *Star Wars* without special effects.

The Drifters presented Leiber and Stoller with the opportunity to define their production apart from their songwriting. The resultant heady mix of R&B, pop, classical strings, and exotic Latin rhythms opened the door for everything from Philly soul to progressive rock, and handed Phil Spector the blueprint for his entire career. Working with material from Doc Pomus and Mort Shuman, Gerry Goffin and Carole King, Burt Bacharach and Hal David, and Barry Mann and Cynthia Weil, Leiber and Stoller proved themselves as savvy with new songs from other writers as with their own, and as adept with drama as with comedy.

From the sparkly girl-group pop of the Dixie Cups' "Chapel of Love" to the spare, swampy soul of Alvin Robinson's "Down Home Girl," from the Brechtian cabaret of Peggy Lee's "Is That All There Is?" to the Celtic country-funk of Stealers Wheel's "Stuck in the Middle with You," Leiber and Stoller approached each production individually, rather than as part of a monolithic body of work. Each act was a new cast; each song was a new script. Even when they didn't write the songs, they still wrote the records.

The list of the records they wrote can be found online at www.leiberstoller.com/Productions.html.

Acknowledgments

Mike and Jerry's

In memory of Lester Sill

with many thanks to:
David Ritz
Randy Poe
Marilyn Levy
Peter Stoller
Emma Sweeney

David's

Mike & Jerry, for giving me this great gig & being
    wonderful collaborators
Bob Bender
David Rosenthal
David Vigliano
Geoff Martin
Johanna Li
Roberta, Alison, Jessica, Charlotte, Alden, James, Henry,
    Jim, Elizabeth, Pops Ritz, and my entire loving family
Alan Eisenstock, Hurry Weinger

Credits

All Songs Written by Jerry Leiber and Mike Stoller Except Where Noted

administered by Sony/ATV Music Publishing LLC, 8 Music Square West, Nashville, TN 37203. All rights reserved. Used by permission.

Shoppin' For Clothes Words and Music by Jerry Leiber, Mike Stoller, and Kent Harris © 1960 Sony/ATV Music Publishing LLC and Five Points Music. All rights administered by Sony/ATV Music Publishing LLC, 8 Music Square West, Nashville, TN 37203. All rights reserved. Used by permission.

Spanish Harlem Words and Music by Jerry Leiber and Phil Spector © 1960, 1961 Sony/ATV Music Publishing LLC and Mother Bertha Music, Inc. Copyrights renewed. All rights on behalf of Sony/ATV Music Publishing LLC administered by Sony/ATV Music Publishing LLC, 8 Music Square West, Nashville, TN 37203. Alll rights on behalf of Mother Bertha Music, Inc., controlled and administered by EMI April Music, Inc. International copyright secured. All rights reserved. Used by permission.

I'm A Woman; Little Egypt © 1961 Sony/ATV Music Publishing LLC. All rights administered by Sony/ATV Music Publishing LLC, 8 Music Square West, Nashville, TN 37203. All rights reserved. Used by permission.

Stand By Me Words and Music by Jerry Leiber, Mike Stoller, and Ben E. King © 1961 Sony/ATV Music Publishing LLC. All rights administered by Sony/ATV Music Publishing LLC, 8 Music Square West, Nashville, TN 37203. All rights reserved. Used by permission.

Bossa Nova Baby © 1963 Sony/ATV Music Publishing LLC. All rights administered by Sony/ATV Music Publishing LLC, 8 Music Square West, Nashville, TN 37203. All rights reserved. Used by permission.

Only In America Words and Music by Jerry Leiber, Mike Stoller, Barry Mann and Cynthia Weil © 1963 (Renewed 1991) SCREEN GEMS-EMI MUSIC INC. All rights reserved. International copyright secured. Used by permission.

Brother Bill (The Last Clean Shirt) Words and Music by Jerry Leiber, Mike Stoller, and Charles Otis © 1964 Jerome Leiber Music, Purple Starfish Music. All rights administered by Sony/ATV Music Publishing LLC, 8 Music Square West, Nashville, TN 37203. All rights reserved. Used by permission.

Photo Credits

Pp. x, 41, 72, 87, 104, 110, 113, 115, 117, 118, 123, 137, 139, 158, 173, 180, 244, 262, 283, 288: Courtesy of the Leiber & Stoller Archives

Pp. 4, 8, 23, 26, 192, 225, 289: Private collection of Mike Stoller

Pp. 6, 11, 155, 193, 280, 287: Private collection of Jerry Leiber

Pp. 42, 58, 62, 92, 147, 178: Michael Ochs Archives/Getty Images

P. 125: Elvis image used by permission, Elvis Presley Enterprises, Inc.

P. 164: Photo by Arne Norlin, courtesy of the Leiber & Stoller Archives

P. 223: Photo by William Claxton

P. 273: Photo by Martien van Beeck

P. 283: Courtesy of the photographer, Leonardo de Vega

P. 288: Photo by Dan Budnik

Index

Note: Page numbers in *italics* refer to illustrations. Song titles are by Leiber and Stoller unless otherwise noted.